Literacy in the Mountains

Literacy in the Mountains

Community, Newspapers, and Writing in Appalachia

Samantha NeCamp

UNIVERSITY PRESS OF KENTUCKY

Scholarly publisher for the Commonwealth,
serving Bellarmine University, Berea College, Centre College of Kentucky, Eastern Kentucky University, The Filson Historical Society, Georgetown College, Kentucky Historical Society, Kentucky State University, Morehead State University, Murray State University, Northern Kentucky University, Transylvania University, University of Kentucky, University of Louisville, and Western Kentucky University.

Editorial and Sales Offices: The University Press of Kentucky
663 South Limestone Street, Lexington, Kentucky 40508-4008
www.kentuckypress.com

Library of Congress Cataloging-in-Publication Data

Names: NeCamp, Samantha, author.
Title: Literacy in the mountains : community, newspapers, and writing in Appalachia / Samantha NeCamp.
Description: Lexington : University Press of Kentucky, 2020. | Series: Place matters: New directions in Appalachian studies | Includes bibliographical references and index.
Identifiers: LCCN 2019045521 | ISBN 9780813178851 (hardcover) | ISBN 9780813178882 (pdf) | ISBN 9780813178875 (epub)
Subjects: LCSH: Literacy—Appalachian Region—History. | Education—Appalachian Region—History.
Classification: LCC LC5147.A67 N44 2020 | DDC 372.6—dc23
LC record available at https://lccn.loc.gov/2019045521

This book is printed on acid-free paper meeting the requirements of the American National Standard for Permanence in Paper for Printed Library Materials.

Manufactured in the United States of America

Member of the Association of University Presses

Contents

Introduction 1

1. Recovering Literacy: A Case for the News as Archive 13

2. Sponsoring Literacy in Appalachia 26

3. Writing a Community 49

4. Schooling Appalachia 73

Conclusion 94

Acknowledgments 113

Notes 115

Bibliography 127

Index 137

Introduction

In the months prior to the 2016 presidential election, correspondents from a wide variety of news outlets began to filter into Appalachia in search of an explanation for the region's supposed support of Donald Trump. Who were these strange people, their articles pondered, who thought that a reality TV star was the best of all possible candidates? Despite Trump's widespread support in many traditionally Republican states—as well as his support in purple Michigan, Wisconsin, and Pennsylvania—Appalachia became the testing ground for theories about his appeal and the perceived epicenter of his support. It was, as one reported dubbed it, "the symbolic heart of Trump's white working-class base."[1]

Some reporters who sought to examine Appalachia prior to the election—labeling it, more often than not, *Trump Country*—offered portraits of the area with at least an attempt at sympathetic representation of its citizens. Yet a common trope in even the most respectful efforts frequently described the residents in terms of how different they are from the rest of America. Roger Cohen, writing for the *New York Times*, for instance, explains Trump's success by appealing to the supposed universal values of Appalachia: "Trump's perceived character—a strong leader with a simple message, never flinching from a fight, cutting through political correctness with a bracing bluntness—resonates in places like Appalachia, where courage, country, and cussedness are core values." Cohen goes on to represent Kentucky—its Appalachian portion in particular—explicitly as the "other" of civilized society: "For anyone used to New York chatter, or for that matter London or Paris chatter, Kentucky is a through-the-looking-glass experience." Similarly, Jeff Saward, writing for *Vanity Fair*, attempts to project sympathy and understanding for West Virginians who plan to vote for Trump—but by accusing them of a willing lack of taste. "You may wonder," he says to the reader, "How could someone vote for a man so resistant to grace, to convention, to good taste? And those people will tell you, look where good taste brought us." Appalachia is Trump Country, then, precisely because it is the opposite of the tasteful, respectable confines of the rest of the United States.[2]

Such descriptions are very common. As Ronald Eller has explained: "The 'idea of Appalachia' has played a counterpoint to the idea of America." This "idea of Appalachia" encompasses poverty, ignorance, isolation, coal wars, and bloody feuds, and it signifies, more than anything, "the place where the American dream ha[s] failed." The 2016 news stories about Appalachia highlight this failure, emphasizing the loss of coal jobs and the resulting poverty as well as the opioid epidemic. *The Guardian*, for instance, visited Beattyville, Kentucky, in 2016 because, according to the US Census, it is "America's poorest white town," "blighted by a lack of jobs and addiction to painkillers." The town is chosen for attention precisely because of its extremes, its difference in relation to the rest of the United States.[3]

Prior to the election, the othering of Appalachia in recent years had taken a largely pitying approach. Its residents are different, the story goes, but in a benign and curious fashion, echoing Wallace Harney's nineteenth-century description of the region as a "strange land and peculiar people." In the aftermath of the election, the attention continued, but now in the form of either think pieces that represented continued support for the president as akin to a mental illness or more direct attacks depicting the region and its voters as threats to the nation. The staff of the Daily Kos suggested, for instance, that former coal miners in Appalachia deserved to lose their health insurance because they had chosen to vote overwhelmingly for the GOP. In a *New York Magazine* article tellingly titled "No Sympathy for the Hillbilly," Frank Rich argues that Democrats should give up on white rural Trump voters: "Let Trump's white working-class base take responsibility for its own votes . . . and live with the election's consequences. . . . That they will sabotage other needy Americans along with them is unavoidable." In other words, according to this narrative, Appalachians screwed us all. Trump is terrible, and the people to blame for Trump are, very specifically, hillbillies: white, rural people from central Appalachia, to the exclusion of other voters who chose Trump. The implication here, of course, is that Appalachians are ignorant for voting against their perceived interests. That ignorance was seen as simply quaint when Hillary Clinton's victory was a foregone conclusion—akin, one might say, to a freak show at a circus (or, per Roger Cohen, the Red Queen's kingdom). In postelection examinations of the area, that ignorance becomes a danger to the nation as a whole.[4]

This image should have collided with the reality that most Trump voters were not members of the working class. The idea that hillbillies—figured as rural, working-class and poor whites—were the sole or even primary reason that Trump was elected, then, is an inaccurate argument. Indeed, we might more aptly criticize Appalachians in particular as *too apathetic* about the results of the election, given the low voter turnout in the region. In McDowell County, West Virginia, which the reporter Elizabeth Hagedorn dubbed "the most pro-Trump county in America," Trump did receive 74.7 percent of the vote. But that number becomes less telling when we realize that only 36.4 percent of eligible voters in McDowell County went to the polls on Election Day. That is to say, 63.6 percent of registered voters did not cast a vote for anyone, and an additional 8.2 percent of registered voters cast their votes for Clinton. Only 26.3 percent of McDowell County voters actually chose to vote for Trump—hardly a tidal wave of support. Yet these voters—just over four thousand people—are held up as destroying not just the lives of their fellow Appalachians but the lives of *all* Americans through their actions on Election Day. In the popular narrative, their ignorance is a weapon turned against the rest of the country.[5]

Given these statistics, it is difficult to understand the blame heaped on Appalachia for Trump's election. I argue that this strange scapegoating occurs because, in the simplest terms, it already has a history of occurring. As Kim Donehower explains: "Since the late nineteenth century, many Americans have seemed to need Appalachia to be a certain way to justify their own worldviews." We can see this in current critiques: behind many of the harshest attacks on Appalachia lies a sense that Appalachians are fools for thinking they can escape their history. Kevin Baker, writing for the *New Republic* about McDowell County, declares: "The people of Trump Country, like so much of white America, long for a past that never was, and a future that cannot be. A past cleansed of conflict, where a big, paternalistic company gave them nice things if they worked hard. A future where, who knows, maybe an orange-haired grifter really *will* restore everything to the way it allegedly was back in their parents' time because . . . well, because he said he would." In other words, Baker sees these Appalachian voters—who are at a Bernie Sanders town hall, it is worth noting—as gullible fools taken in by a con man precisely because they are unfamiliar with their own history of economic exploitation. These people, he suggests, don't seem to realize that they've always been poor, poorly educated rubes. They actually think they used to amount to something.[6]

In one sense, Baker is right. Not many people have an accurate sense of historical Appalachia: the image on which Baker and his fellow Trump Country reporters trade is assumed to be the reality, but very little evidence is presented to support that interpretation. As Ronald Lewis explains, the continued force of these stereotypes exists in part because "so little formal written history about preindustrial Appalachia exists to provide a measure of empirical authenticity." Similarly, Mary Beth Pudup, Dwight Billings, and Altina Waller explain that "knowledge of preindustrial Appalachia has more often than not been based solely on discursive knowledge of an intertextual reality (the myth of Appalachia) rather than historical knowledge of an actual place," a point I return to below. In the absence of such evidence, myths create our assumptions about Appalachia. In particular, Baker and Rich are both harking back to the idea of Appalachia. As Shapiro explains: "Between 1870 and 1900, it became clear . . . that the existence of a strange land and peculiar people in the southern mountains could not be understood in terms of contemporary conceptions of America as a unified and homogeneous national entity." This was not, Shapiro argues, because Appalachia had always been a distinct region or because it was distinctly different from many other rural areas of the country; rather, it was a result of changing perceptions about what it meant to be an American, perceptions driven by the need to reunify after the Civil War, racial upheaval, and second-wave immigration. As Shapiro puts it: "What had seemed normal or at least explicable came after 1870 to seem nonnormal and inexplicable." I have argued elsewhere that, with the dawn of second-wave immigration, it became necessary to define *American* in very particular ways in order to identify and neutralize the threat posed by the newcomers, a process facilitated by a burgeoning national press and the ever-increasing interconnectedness of the nation. Appalachia did not fit neatly into this narrative, but this allowed the region to serve an important purpose: it became part of the other against which America defined itself. As John Williams explains, Appalachia became an "'alternative America' projected onto the mountains and mountain people by reformers whose real purpose is to critique or change things in the nation at large." This othering fostered the idea of Appalachia as an area rife with illiteracy and generally opposed to educational opportunities, an area of blood feuds and violence, of poverty and ignorance.[7]

Appalachia's illiteracy is a long-standing literary and cultural trope, even among scholars. It has been featured in some of the earliest research in what we would now consider literacy studies. In their groundbreaking study of literacy and schooling, for instance, Lee Soltow and Edward Stevens employ Appalachia as a limiting case against which to weigh their findings, citing its "extremes of illiteracy, an absence of centralized authority, and a lack of social concentration," and describing the region as trapped in a "vicious cycle of illiteracy, immobility, and lack of economic opportunity." This trope is repeated over time by commentators from a variety of fields. In 1947, the historian Arnold Toynbee described Appalachians as having "relapsed into illiteracy and witchcraft." In 1971, the psychologist David Looff asserted that Appalachians "place little value on verbal skills" and "dislike . . . regular schooling." Cora Wilson Stewart, the founder of the Moonlight Schools, an adult literacy education program, often highlighted the "scarcity of interesting books in [the] locality." In his 1898 novel *The Kentuckians*, John Fox Jr., perhaps the strongest force behind the development of the idea of Appalachia, describes eastern Kentucky as textless: "Put twenty *average* blue-grass families down in the mountains half a dozen miles from one another, take away their books, keep them there, with no schools and no churches, for a hundred years, and they will be as ignorant and lawless as the mountaineer."[8]

Scholarship in Appalachian studies has long since illustrated that the representation of Appalachia as a backward, isolated, and immobile place in the nineteenth century is inaccurate, and many historians examined the emergence of the idea of Appalachia in local color writing beginning in the 1880s. As I have argued elsewhere, however, relatively little research has sought to address specifically the (un)reality of Appalachian illiteracy in the nineteenth century and the early twentieth—to respond directly to the representations of Appalachia as an illiterate, unschooled, textless society. This is in large part because so little archival evidence exists through which to document literacy practices in the region.[9]

This lack, taken at face value, might suggest that no such materials ever existed. Several factors, however, play into this dearth. One factor is eminently practical. While buildings—particularly public buildings—were often constructed of stone or brick in many areas of the country, in Appalachia wood was more commonly used. Thus, fires consuming courthouses, for instance, have destroyed many historical records. The phenomenon is so common, in fact, that the Kentucky Department of Archives and Libraries website features a page titled "County Courthouse Disasters in Kentucky." For example, Wolfe County, one of the research sites in this study, saw its courthouse burn twice—in 1886 and again in 1913—destroying all county records of prior years. Another reason for the lack of archival evidence is the upheaval in the region wrought by the extract industry. With the development of coal and timber camps, Appalachians were in motion: many people left traditional family homes to move into the coal camps, and, when one coal seam played out, families might move to another camp. This motion discouraged, as it does among all migrants, the accumulation of documents that needed to be transported. Appalachians, then, were less likely to maintain the ephemera that more sedentary communities might find stored away in an attic.[10]

The final, more insidious reason is that Appalachians are *assumed to be illiterate.* This assumption has limited the value placed on documents produced in Appalachia. Donehower explains: "When it comes to qualitative research on Appalachian literacy . . . all participants in the equation—the researchers, the researched, and the readers of the research produced—are subject to strong sociocultural and psychological forces that might affect their abilities to write, speak, and read about Appalachian literacy in accurate and ethical ways." Similar sociocultural and psychological forces have in the past affected historians and librarians who might have been in a position to preserve data about Appalachia. If we have been immersed in a world that sees Appalachia as an illiterate, textless region, we are preconditioned to overlook and devalue the texts we encounter there. Until scholarly interest in Appalachia bloomed in the late twentieth century, texts from the region were not hoarded and collected; librarians did not often seek out these materials for collection. Similarly, residents themselves did not see their own writing as something that needed to be kept for posterity. Sara Webb-Sunderhaus writes: "We [Appalachians] grow accustomed to seeing ourselves (and our literacies) through our own eyes as well as the eyes of others. Those eyes are not often kind."[11]

In most cases, our knowledge of the literacy practices of past communities reflects the extent to which those communities valued their own practices and saw their productions as products to pass on. As Jennifer Sinor puts it: "In determining the values of a society, you need only investigate what gets discarded." Appalachians—at least from the late nineteenth century on—were trained to think of themselves as producing no written work of particular value. It is not surprising, then, that relatively few documents have survived to attest to the day-to-day literacy practices of their communities.[12]

Beyond these somewhat benign explanations, too, lies the history that has been deliberately discarded, bulldozed over, or blown up along with the mountaintops of the area. The site of the Battle of Blair Mountain, in Logan County, West Virginia (discussed at greater length below) is instructive in this regard. The battle is considered by many historians to be the largest labor uprising in US history, its site one that many would consider essential to understanding the story of America. However, a debate currently rages about whether to include the site on the National Register of Historic Places, run by the National Park Service. The problem with such a designation is that the land is currently owned by Alpha Natural Resources and Arch Coal, which have received permits allowing mountaintop removal coal mining on the site. When the site was listed by the Park Service, the companies filed suit to have the designation removed and falsely told local residents "that they would lose their land if the battlefield were listed." The site was then delisted from the National Register, according to a judge in the case, "at the urging of coal companies owning land on Blair Mountain." Currently, the case is in the courts, and mountaintop removal is on hold, but ongoing clear-cutting of timber on the site has already destroyed some of the historical features. Even though, as Bill Price of the Sierra Club puts it, "It would be a disaster to blow up a mountain of such significance. It would be like blowing up Gettysburg," the site could be reopened for detonation at any moment. Blair Mountain, then, is perhaps the most dramatic example, but it is not particularly unique: Appalachian history, particularly when it is a history of rising up against local conditions, is very often deliberately obfuscated, downplayed, or destroyed in the name of supporting economic progress.[13]

The absence of the historical documents that would help illustrate the pre- and early industrial history of Appalachia has left a blank space in our understanding, and, in its place, we are left with myths that were first articulated by writers and industrialists who aimed to present the region as in need of intervention—intervention they were only too happy to provide, for their own profit. Today, as Ronald Eller explains, the perpetuation of these negative images places blame for Appalachia's continued poverty squarely on its inhabitants and "allow[s] the rest of America to keep the region at arm's length, rather than to confront the systemic problems of a dependent economy, environmental decay, and institutional weakness that challenge mountain communities today." This lacuna in our sense of what Appalachia has been influences our view of who Appalachians are and can be. If, as Baker would have it, Appalachians have *always been* the fools exploited by corporate interests, and if they've *always* been too ignorant to act in their own interest, how can they (and, in this imagining, Appalachians are a unified cultural entity) be anything other than ignorant, exploited fools? Any choices made, any support given, any future envisioned is refracted through the lens of this imagined past.[14]

The mythology surrounding Appalachia became a self-fulfilling prophecy. It is impossible to deny, for instance, the truth of *The Guardian's* central premise: Appalachia is indeed less economically prosperous than much of the rest of the country. Educational opportunities are decreasing, with school districts in the area on the verge of bankruptcy owing to the loss of coal industry tax dollars. On nearly any map detailing success, Appalachia stands out as an outlier. However, this reality is the result of specific historical choices—choices based on the idea of Appalachia—rather than the inevitable result of "cyclic poverty," as Soltow and Stevens would have it. Another way to put it is that the American Dream did not simply fail in the region—it was deliberately killed, and the creation of a false history of the region characterized by ignorance, textlessness, illiteracy, and poverty was one of the tools used to murder it.[15]

Filling these gaps in our historical knowledge, then, may play a small role in changing current perceptions and, by extension, future possibilities for Appalachians. As Yuval Noah Harari explains, we study history "to understand that our present situation is neither natural nor inevitable, and that we consequently have many more possibilities before us than we imagine." Imagining new perceptions and possibilities for Appalachians requires us to turn to a historical period before current stereotypes were cemented and recover, as much as possible, Appalachians' representations of themselves as readers and writers.[16]

The Project

To that end, this book seeks to recover perhaps the only extensive archive of Appalachians' representations of their own literacy practices in the period during which the idea of Appalachia was first articulated and the takeover of Appalachia by extract industries was beginning—roughly 1885 to 1920. That archive comes in the form of local newspapers preserved by community libraries and digitized by the Chronicling America project. Given the dearth of other kinds of archival material, local newspapers published in Appalachia provide a unique window into the reading and writing practices of the community.

Beyond their desirability as simply the most complete archive available, newspapers provide a unique window into community practices. Alexis de Tocqueville argues that newspapers "maintain civilization" because "nothing but a newspaper can drop the same thought into a thousand minds at the same moment." In his study of the development of nationalism, Benedict Anderson highlights the newspaper's essential role in the creation of an *imagined community*, which he defines as one in which the members "will never know most of their fellow-members, meet them, or even hear of them, yet in the minds of each lives the image of their communion." Newspapers are essential to this communion because they serve as "this extraordinary mass ceremony: the almost precisely simultaneous consumption ('imagining') of the newspaper-as-fiction": "[This ceremony] is performed in silent privacy. . . . Yet each communicant is well aware that the ceremony he performs is being replicated simultaneously by thousands (or millions) of others of whose existence he is confident, yet of whose identity he has not the slightest notion." The newspaper, then—at least historically, prior to the invention of television or the Internet—is one of the essential ingredients in building a shared communal consciousness across spaces too wide to allow for regular physical encounters. The newspaper allowed the development of a sense of shared interests, histories, and experiences all of which encouraged readers to imagine themselves as members of a larger group, as a part of something bigger than their immediate surroundings.[17]

Owing to this role in community creation, newspapers represent a unique window into community literacy practices. As Anderson and Tocqueville suggest, the newspapers give us a window into what reading experiences a community shared on a given day. In addition, they also give us a window into what products were sold, what meetings were held, which schools were succeeding and which were failing. In short, they present a portrait of the community, one that is not necessarily a full accounting (as I discuss further in chapter 2), but does represent the community *as it imagined itself.* We see not only the actual practices of literacy at work but also the act of bringing into being a community around those practices. This relationship between community building and literacy practices was widely recognized and practiced in the nineteenth century and the early twentieth. Jessica Enoch, for instance, demonstrates how teachers writing for *La Crónica* used that newspaper to provide a rhetorical education to their readers—readers who understood the newspaper as a potential site for such instruction. James Parins has described the role of newspapers in fostering literacy in the Cherokee nation. Similarly, Alicia Brazeau illustrates that "periodicals were commonly viewed as both a form of entertainment and a tool for literacy learning." Each of these studies makes clear that newspaper readers and writers across the country understood the newspaper as a community of literacy practices, one that formed around negotiation of what kinds of literacy were most appropriate and effective. Throughout my examination of the newspapers, I consider how they create the kind of imagined community that Anderson and Tocqueville invoke—a community that exists only on paper but one that tells us much about and that influences the physical communities in which its members take part.[18]

The creation of the imagined community via the newspaper places a great deal of power in the hands of a single community member: the editor. Indeed, editors in the small weeklies of the Appalachian region had even more power than we would typically ascribe to an editor because almost all were also the owners and primary writers for their papers. Few had more than one additional staff member. In other words, the editor had complete control over copy. As such, editors in Appalachia functioned as what Deborah Brandt has termed *sponsors of literacy*, which she defines as "any agents, local or distant, concrete or abstract, who enable, support, teach, model, as well as recruit, regulate, suppress, or withhold literacy—and gain advantage by it in some way." She goes on to suggest that "sponsors are delivery systems for the economies of literacy." In the case of Appalachian newspaper editors, this delivery was quite literal: they saw to it that the written word and the imagined community arrived at subscribers' doorsteps once per week. But their role as sponsors went beyond simply producing the written word: they took an active role in shaping the imagined community, both in their choices of what materials were included in the paper and in their explicit discussions of appropriate literacy practices within the community (which I discuss further in chapter 2). They also provided the space and the readership for writers from the imagined community, encouraging local men and women to become correspondents for the paper (which I discuss further in chapter 3).[19]

While the editor played an outsized role in the creation of the imagined community, it should be noted that, as Brandt says, all sponsors "enter a reciprocal relationship with those they underwrite." Editors provided the space and the material, but, ultimately, they were dependent on the reading public for their economic survival. The historian George Payne illustrates that editors made their income primarily from advertising; however, to procure advertisements, they had to be able to demonstrate a healthy subscriber list and maintain a positive position in the community. Today, we often see advertisers flee controversial television programming; similarly, advertisers in the past were leery of associating themselves with unpopular newspapers. Editors, then, were beholden to the very imagined community that their newspapers helped instantiate; fail to meet community expectations, and the paper itself might fail, to be replaced by a different iteration. The newspapers demonstrate this reciprocal relationship well, with letters to the editor and editorial responses illustrating the push and pull of the imagined community enforcing its norms on all involved in these literacy transactions.[20]

Drawing on the newspaper as archive, we can recover literacy practices in Appalachia in three distinct ways. First, the newspapers provide direct access to reading and writing practices via community contributions: local correspondence makes up much of the content of newspapers of the period, allowing us direct access to the writings of community members as well as, in those writings, individuals' accounts of their own reading experiences—particularly how they read the newspaper itself. Second, the literacy artifacts within the paper illustrate how literacy sponsorship worked both to channel and to respond to literacy practices within the community. The editors' choices regarding what to include within their papers illustrates their visions of appropriate reading and writing practices. Advertisements within the papers speak to what outsiders believed about the communities' literacy practices; a company would not waste money, for instance, advertising lengthy tomes to a community believed to be largely illiterate, so the presence of particular kinds of advertisements tells us much about the assumptions outsiders held about the region. Finally, representations of educational practices in the news help us evaluate the truth of Looff's claim that Appalachians placed little value on schooling and, by extension, the school-based literacies sponsored in educational settings.

The Plan of the Book

The goal of this book is to respond to calls for a rounder historical portrait of Appalachia by utilizing weekly newspapers as a historical archive of literacy practices. In particular, the book is intended to respond to the idea of Appalachia, with a focus on disrupting the idea that Appalachians were illiterate, textless, and unschooled. I begin this project, in chapter 1, by outlining the rationale for choosing the five newspapers featured in this study as representative texts and explaining how I identified representations of literacy within them. In chapter 2, I discuss the role of the editors as sponsors of literacy, examining their efforts to cultivate an imagined community of readers. Using Brandt's definition of *sponsorship*, I illustrate the ways in which the editors taught, modeled, and regulated literacy via discussions of appropriate reading and writing practices. In this chapter, I also discuss how advertisements for texts of all kinds debunk the idea of a textless Appalachia, and I discuss what the editors' choices of advertisement suggest about how they imagined their audiences.

In chapter 3, I turn to community writing, the most direct evidence in the paper of community literacy practices. Because each paper relied on local correspondents to write in with news from far-flung communities, the correspondent columns offer a glimpse into what local writers viewed as particularly important events. While many of the events covered are what we might expect from a typical correspondent column—births, illnesses, marriages, deaths—there is ample representation of literacy practices, and the attention with which these are reported suggests the value placed on literacy in these communities. I also consider how the correspondents interacted with one another and with the editor, with the editor in this case serving as a *recruiter* and an *enabler* of literacy, to use Brandt's terms, but also as a suppressor who ultimately exercised control over what correspondents could say in print.

In chapter 4, I turn my attention specifically to schooling, which features in many of the correspondent columns as well as in pieces written by the editors. In particular, the papers illustrate that a thriving industry of ad hoc private schooling institutions was active in eastern Kentucky, a fact very seldom recognized in histories of the area. While modern studies of schooling and literacy frequently cite public school data to suggest that Kentuckians were unsupportive of schooling, the newspapers demonstrate that many of these supposedly unschooled children were in fact receiving an education from privately run institutions that some of the editors touted as superior to that received in the public schools. The newspapers also demonstrate the vibrant community support for education, belying the myth of a people resistant to schooling.

To close, I return to present-day perceptions of Appalachia to illustrate the ongoing harm caused by the persistence of stereotypes regarding Appalachians' literacy practices. By reframing Appalachian history, we can begin to see that, while the current circumstances in the region are indeed a product of history, they are not a product of the history presented in popular narratives—narratives that attribute any negative development in Appalachia to the natural consequence of the region's long-standing poverty and ignorance. Recovering Appalachians' literacy history gives us a new lens through which to examine our experiences, expectations, and potential futures.

1

Recovering Literacy

A Case for the News as Archive

As discussed in the previous chapter, this project aims to identify newspapers that will allow us to recover representations of literacy practices in Appalachia. As in any project involving representation, many competing factors influenced how this one could be conceptualized. What counts as Appalachia? What time period is most important to recover? What newspapers are most representative of the production of news and the enactment of literacy in the mountains? In this chapter, I attempt to grapple with these questions and outline my rationale for the choices made in this project. I have attempted to identify how my choices succeed and fail to represent a sense of Appalachia as a distinct community at a particular point in its history.

Because my goal is to interrogate the myth of Appalachia as illiterate and textless, I opted to focus on texts that represented the period of time during which these myths were first articulated. The idea of Appalachia, as Henry Shapiro and Alan Batteau have argued, emerged initially from the work of local color writers who presented the region as the other of civilized America. It was built on by newspaper editors, politicians, and reformers throughout the country, not coincidentally, just as the extract industries began to seek out opportunities in the region. Richard Drake explains that many of the "explorers" of the region in the 1880s doubled as industrial promoters, citing the Louisville newspaper editor Henry Watterson as one such example. It is difficult to pinpoint a specific year in which the extract industries began to have an outsized effect on the Appalachian economy, but Drake points out that buyers purchasing mineral rights from central Appalachians first arrived in the 1880s alongside those same local color writers, explorers, and industrial promoters, illustrating the tight linkage between the creation of the idea of Appalachia and the industries that would exploit that image. Any attempt to recover Appalachian literacy practices, then, should begin at least with this period since it is at this time that the myth of Appalachian *illiteracy* first took root.[1]

For the purposes of this project, then, I begin searching for Appalachian literacy practices in 1885, the year after the publication of the first local color book to be set entirely in Appalachia, Mary Noailles Murfree's *In the Tennessee Mountains*, brought the idea of Appalachia into northern homes. Locating an end point for such a study is more difficult as the myths continue to hold power today. However, since I am particularly interested in the period in which the idea of Appalachia was being articulated and gaining its cultural currency, I aimed for the time when this myth became fully accepted as incontrovertible fact—the time when it became nearly impossible to imagine Appalachia as anything else. While arguments could be made for several dates, I take as the end point the gunfight of May 1920 in Matewan, West Virginia, the subsequent trial of those involved, and the Battle of Blair Mountain in 1921 as providing the closing date for the acceptance of the idea of Appalachia. The death during the gunfight in Matewan of seven Baldwin-Felts agents hired by mining companies helped thrust Appalachia fully into the national spotlight; the trial of the sheriff, Sid Hatfield, accused of gunning down the agents was a spectacle covered by every major newspaper of the day. Hatfield's subsequent murder by Baldwin-Felts agents was the spark needed to touch off armed conflict between miners working to maintain a union and the coal companies and their supporters, a conflict that culminated in the use of federal troops at the Battle of Blair Mountain to break up the striking miners' forces. At this moment, I argue, the power of the idea of Appalachia was cemented: when the government intervened to support the coal companies' exploitative policies following the murder—in broad daylight, on the courthouse steps—of a popular elected figure representing the miners, it served as nothing less than an endorsement of the image of Appalachians as ignorant, violent hillbillies who needed to be put in their place at any cost. Given the national attention garnered by this series of events, it certainly became difficult to forward an alternative to this narrative in the aftermath. Thus, I take 1920 as an end point for my study of Appalachian literacy practices.[2]

With this time period in mind, I then looked for newspapers that were most representative of the area particularly impugned by the idea of Appalachia—namely, central Appalachia. While the Appalachian Regional Commission (ARC) designates "420 counties in 13 states" as part of the Appalachian region, in cultural terms Delaware County, New York—about 150 miles outside New York City—does not carry the same baggage as Pike County, Kentucky, or Mingo County, West Virginia. I narrowed my focus to those areas designated by the ARC and others as central Appalachia, a region encompassing Kentucky's Appalachian counties (roughly the eastern third of the state), western West Virginia and Virginia, and northeastern Tennessee. It is this region that is most associated with local color writing and the extract industries, and, in modern times, it is this region that, not coincidentally, neatly matches the map of economically distressed counties issued by the ARC. This region has borne the brunt of the idea of Appalachia, and it is here that we most need to recover a history of literacy practices in order to combat that image. I also attended to potential objections, the most pressing of which was that if I selected newspapers located in border counties—those that touched neighboring counties not considered Appalachian—the evidence of literacy might be taken as more representative of the flatland readership than of the Appalachian subscribers. To respond to this potential, I searched for newspapers based in interior counties surrounded entirely by other Appalachian counties.[3]

Because the local news in the era of my study was very much *local news*—that is, news of events and people within the immediate area rather than national reporting—I decided to limit my focus to a single state. I opted to focus my attention in this way in order to better understand how the peculiarities of various state laws—particularly those related to education—were understood and adapted at the local level. A state-based focus also provided a unique window into politics as papers of different political persuasions endorsed or reviled particular candidates and policy proposals at the state level. With my criteria for date and location in mind, the only state that represented a viable option at the time of this study was Kentucky, simply because it was the only state boasting several newspapers fitting the geographic profile I have described that had a significant number of extant digitized issues.

However, I recognize that, in focusing on a single state, I am courting two potential concerns. First, I may be limiting the scope of my findings—that these results may not be representative of the larger Appalachian region. Second, I may be perpetuating the very stereotypes I seek to displace by presenting Appalachia as a homogeneous region in which one area is exactly the same as another. As John Williams reminds us, there are many doubts "about whether or not the findings of specific historical, ethnographic, and sociological case studies extend to Appalachia as a whole." Williams himself characterizes an area roughly corresponding to the ARC designation of central Appalachia as a core region almost universally recognized by Appalachian scholars as definably Appalachian in nature, sharing many social as well as geographic characteristics. However, he argues that, rather than thinking of Appalachia as a region defined by natural boundaries, it is more useful to think of it as a "zone of interaction among diverse peoples who have lived in or acted upon it, as it is also of their interactions with the region's complex environment"—a zone that is in some ways unique in its characteristics but that exchanges many of its characteristics with surrounding areas as well.[4]

This idea—that Appalachia is both distinct from and interwoven within a larger state and national context—is essential for dismantling the stereotypes of the region. By choosing Kentucky, I recognize that I risk perpetuating the idea that there are "two Kentuckies," a concept first articulated by James Lane Allen in his work for *Harper's Weekly*—a division typically used to mark the Appalachian section of the state as a land apart from and (in every way) behind the Bluegrass region of the state. Rather, I chose to focus on a single state to illustrate, in part, that the kinds of literacy practices present in this region differ very little from those that we might find in newspapers from any region of any state of the country. While certain features of the political system or geographic settings may differ, what this study intends to illustrate is that the areas studied are not particularly distinct from other areas—that the dichotomies on which the idea of Appalachia trades are, as Williams suggests, simply not there. Instead, the geographic region depicted in these newspapers illustrates that Appalachia is indeed better conceived of as a zone of interaction rather than a "strange land and peculiar people."[5]

The newspapers I have selected are themselves such zones of interaction; within their pages, correspondents from locations throughout the mountains, including areas in Kentucky, West Virginia, Virginia, and Tennessee, voice their views on local and regional events. I do not intend to make a claim to universal applicability—the particular conditions of the communities that housed the newspapers were unique and idiosyncratic in many ways. However, the sheer geographic reach of the newspapers via the correspondent columns featured speaks to a widely shared set of interests—what Benedict Anderson calls an *imagined community*. Given this expansive readership, it seems reasonable to believe that the ways in which literacy and schooling are represented in the newspapers reflect widespread attitudes and behaviors within central Appalachia, despite my choice to focus on a single state.[6]

Given these constraints, this study focuses on five papers from eastern Kentucky. I examined the *Breathitt County News*, a short-lived paper in Jackson that ran from 1901 to 1911; the *Hazel Green Herald*, published in

Wolfe County's Hazel Green from 1885 until at least 1917; the *Big Sandy News*, published in Lawrence County's Louisa from 1885 to the present; the *Clay City Times*, originally the *Spout Spring Times*, published in Powell County's Clay City from 1896 to the present; and the *Mountain Advocate*, published in Knox County's Barbourville from 1904 to the present. Nearly all newspapers were at this time politically affiliated, so it's important to note that the *Big Sandy News*, the *Clay City Times*, and the *Hazel Green Herald* were all Democratic papers while the *Mountain Advocate* was Republican and the *Breathitt County News* a uniquely positioned Democratic paper that took a compromised position against the Democratic Party machine and in favor of mostly Republican candidates. I will discuss these papers in more detail below.

In examining these papers, I have read all extant digitized issues for the first three years of the papers' existence. I have focused on the early years because it is during this period that the editors of these papers expend the most effort and page space to create a readership and therefore mostly clearly and explicitly invoke an imagined community of which readers are members. In every case, the editors make an explicit argument within their papers' pages regarding what reading and writing within the community should be—what kinds of reading material were appropriate and what kinds of writing should be engaged in. Among the remaining digitized issues, I have selected one issue per month. In choosing a monthly issue, I have alternated weeks to avoid overemphasizing advertisements that appeared only in specific weeks—for instance, several businesses seem to have placed advertisements only in the first week of each month. I have considered all the material within each issue, including headings, articles, correspondence, and advertisements.[7]

But what is it that we should look for when we look for evidence of literacy? As Harvey Graff cautions us: "Discussions about literacy levels rarely pause to consider what is meant by literacy." The definition of *literacy* is, of course, contested and can be imagined very narrowly, as simply the ability to decode printed text, or quite expansively, as in Paul Prior and Jody Shipka's formulation: "Literate activity is about nothing less than ways of being in the world, forms of life." For my own purposes elsewhere, I would define *literacy* much as Deborah Brandt has, treating "literacy skill . . . primarily as a resource—economic, political, intellectual, spiritual—which, like wealth or education, or trade skill or social connections, is pursued for the opportunity and protections that it potentially grants its seekers." In other words, I view literacy as a form of exchange. In this imagining, "literate abilities originate in social postures and social knowledge that begin well before and extend well beyond words on a page." For the purposes of this study, however, debunking the myth of Appalachia as illiterate, unschooled, and textless demands responding to the myth on its own terms: illustrating that Appalachia is literate, schooled, and text filled. Rather than attempting to read for literacy as more sensitive commentators might define it, then, I focused on evidence that spoke directly to literacy as defined by the myth. When outside commentators reference literacy in Appalachia, they seem to be referring to specifically text-based exchanges that are not everyday—that is, evidence of being able to write a check would not count as evidence of literacy to these commentators. Literacy is reading books, writing letters, attending school: in other words, it is the process of interacting with the kinds of texts deemed valuable in the context of a broad view of American life. Many of those who imagine Appalachia as illiterate point to its lack of text, so I looked for examples of books and other texts in the vicinity—advertisements for books, discussions of libraries and reading clubs, literary criticism, and discussions of the act of writing and its tools (paper, pens, stationary). In reference to Appalachia as unschooled and ignorant, I looked both for evidence of schooling practices and, perhaps more important, for evidence of community attitudes toward schooling. To combat the image of Appalachia as specifically illiterate, I looked for any reference to the acts of reading and writing, with a particular focus on explicit discussions of reading and writing practices and community attitudes about those practices. Thus, I cast my net broadly but remained focused on evidence of specifically (printed) text- or school-oriented literacy practices in each paper over time rather than literacy more broadly conceived. While I noted each instance of these forms of evidence as I read, I am less interested here in presenting a numerical tallying of the presence of literacy than in recovering an overall sense of how an imagined community of readers, writers, and learners developed in the communities these papers served.[8]

The Papers

I turn now to a brief description of the newspapers I selected for this study and the physical communities in which they were located. Although I have chosen these newspapers because of their similarities in geographic location and time frame, each has its own unique milieu and editorial personality. It is important to note these differences as they affect the strategies each editor uses to sponsor his local imagined community.

THE *BIG SANDY NEWS*

Among the newspapers studied here, the *Big Sandy News* is the only paper that was formed from the purchase of another, older paper. The local entrepreneurs Lynn Ferguson and Anderson Webb purchased the *Lawrence County Index* and renamed it the *Big Sandy News*. They seem also to have relocated the paper from elsewhere in the county to the county seat of Louisa, although the details are not fully clear from existing evidence. The change in name is a good indicator of a change in ambition; whereas the previous iteration had been a tiny sheet with low circulation, the *News* aimed to become the source of news for the entire Big Sandy River valley—a goal that was ultimately successful as the *News* features correspondents from many counties on the West Virginia side of the Big Sandy as well as the surrounding Kentucky counties. Despite these lofty goals, Webb was unable to fulfill his commitment to the paper, and after only four issues he sold his share to Milton Conley, a sixteen-year-old former newspaper apprentice, also from Lawrence County. Within two years, Conley also bought Ferguson's share of the paper, making him the sole proprietor and chief writer for the weekly. He would continue this role until 1935. He became one of the most respected newspapermen in the state, and the *Big Sandy News* was named the best country newspaper in Kentucky in 1922. While an active Democrat, Conley did not turn the paper into a militant organ of the party; Democratic talking points are often mentioned, but vitriolic editorials are largely absent. Conley also ran a stationary store out of the *News* building. Because the store sold writing materials and books, including textbooks, it is worth noting that Conley's entire economic identity was built on the foundation of local literacy practices.[9]

The town of Louisa was the largest of the towns featured in this study—the town center held 456 residents and the surrounding precincts approximately 3,500 residents, according to the 1880 Census. The Louisa Normal School was the town's pride and joy, and many articles in the paper feature the happenings there. Because the school was, for many years, one of the town's chief economic drivers as townspeople developed businesses to serve the students, the town itself was also invested in the idea of schooling—after all, not only was the normal school a school itself, but also its role was to train future teachers. Thus, the *News* is more apt to take up issues concerning teacher pay and teacher hiring practices than the other newspapers, presumably because of this local interest.[10]

THE *HAZEL GREEN HERALD*

The *Hazel Green Herald* was also the product of a school town. The Hazel Green Academy was not just the most important but really the only industry in the town of Hazel Green, located in Wolfe County. Unlike some of the other towns featured in this study, Hazel Green was not a county seat, and it is by far the smallest town featured here, with 132 residents listed in the 1880 Census. The surrounding precinct recorded only 1,142 residents. The school and its teachers, then, made up a substantial portion of the town citizenry and activity. The academy was originally founded in 1880 by local businessmen but received a charter and some funding support from the state. By 1886, it was nearly bankrupt and was taken over by the Christian Women's Board of Mission of Kentucky, making it one of the first, if little recognized, sponsored settlement schools in the region. The closest modern analogue to the school would be a private high school, although students could often attend free of charge thanks to the missionary approach to education.[11]

The founder and editor of the *Herald,* Spencer Cooper, arrived in Hazel Green in 1885 after having worked for a local paper in Mt. Sterling, Kentucky, roughly forty miles away. Cooper seems to have chosen Hazel Green because it sat in the middle of an area that was underserved by local papers; as he writes in his first issue, the newspaper "circulates largely in the counties of Wolfe, Morgan, Powell, Menifee, Magoffin, Breathitt, Elliott, Estill, and Floyd, the latter seven being without a newspaper of any kind." Cooper, like the founding editors of the *Big Sandy News*, envisioned a community for his paper that stretched beyond his immediate environs and into adjacent areas. He also showed a firm commitment to education, although, unlike the other editors, he does not place much emphasis on the distinction between public and private schooling—an obvious nod to the fact that a successful private school defined his community. He also makes it more of a point than do other editors to seek out local correspondents from far-flung communities, which speaks to his effort to widen his distribution and subscriber list across a large swath of eastern Kentucky. Like Conley, Cooper was a Democrat and often supported Democratic causes and candidates through the paper. However, party politics did not dominate the news, and editorials explicitly dealing with politics were kept to a minimum. Cooper ran the paper until its closure sometime after 1917 (the date is uncertain;

no archived issues are available beyond 1917); deeply affected by the paper rationing caused by World War I, the *Herald* doesn't seem to have recovered from this economic hit.[12]

THE *MOUNTAIN ADVOCATE*

Like the *Herald* and the *News*, the *Mountain Advocate* was founded in a community centered around education. In the *Advocate's* case, however, it wasn't a matter of a single school defining the community: three noteworthy education institutions were based in Barbourville. Lee's Collegiate Institute and Barbourville Baptist Institute were, like the Hazel Green Academy, essentially equivalent to today's private high schools, designed to prepare young people (mostly, but not entirely, men) for further educational opportunities and careers in lucrative career fields such as law. Union College, a Methodist institution, was, from its earliest days, an institution of higher learning in multiple subject areas, and it drew students from throughout the mountains. Of all the papers, the *Advocate* devotes the most time to higher education, certainly a result of the presence of the college and its faculty among the subscribers.[13]

The *Advocate* was founded in 1904 by Daniel Clark with his brother. The brother's name is never given in the paper, and references to him quickly dwindle away, suggesting that Daniel Clark was, from the outset, the voice of the enterprise. Clark was originally from Georgetown, Kentucky, in the central region of the state; there, his previous paper failed owing to his intensely Republican editorials. Given his history, it is unsurprising that, from the outset, the *Advocate* was much more militant in espousing political views than either the *News* or the *Herald*; scathing editorials directed at Democrats appear frequently, as do endorsements of Republican candidates and positions. Notably, Caleb Powers, a Republican secretary of state accused of complicity in the assassination of Democratic governor William Goebel, became a silent partner in the paper following his pardon in 1908. The intense political stances that Clark (and, later, the other editors) took made Barbourville, with its much more Republican lean, a more appropriate home than Georgetown, despite multiple competing newspapers already present there. That the city was able to support multiple newspapers is slightly surprising, given its relatively small size; the city itself held approximately 450 residents, with an additional 2,200 people in the surrounding precincts. The frequency with which the paper changed hands suggests that the economics of the newspaper were not always in the editor's favor; Clark sold to Charles D. Cole in 1907, who in turn sold to W. H. McDonald in 1909. In 1919, McDonald sold the paper to Fred Burman. Each editor appears loath to undercut the image created by his predecessors. From reading the content alone rather than the byline, it is difficult to pinpoint the moment when editorship changes hands because the content remains essentially the same in tone and focus. Given the effort involved in creating an imagined community and the clearly precarious nature of the enterprise, it stands to reason that each man would do what he could to maintain the existing subscriptions while also occasionally introducing new columns of interest to boost readership.[14]

THE *CLAY CITY TIMES* AND THE *SPOUT SPRING TIMES*

On the other side of the political spectrum, the *Clay City Times* was an intensely Democratic paper, spending much column space on drumming up support for Democratic candidates and, with a tone similar to the *Advocate's,* militantly advocating for Democratic policy issues. The *Clay City Times* was originally the *Spout Spring Times*; the two towns are separated by about four miles but are in different counties. The change in name and location was the result of a fire at the Spout Springs establishment; the nearest suitable replacement building for the print shop and adjoining general store was in Clay City. The seemingly short move was significant in terms of how the paper could frame itself in terms of the competition; while the *Spout Springs Times* was the only paper in its county, Clay City's county was already home to several papers. However, the entire area—Clay City and Spout Springs included—experienced a growth in population near the turn of the century thanks to the logging industry, and the editor seems to have keenly felt the opportunity to cash in on this population.

In my research, I have read all issues of the first three years of both the *Spout Springs Times* and the *Clay City Times*. The editor, J. E. Burgher Jr., uses much the same strategies in both instances to establish his credibility within the community and foster an imagined community, but the *Clay City Times* also draws on the ethos and community developed by the *Spout Spring Times*, allowing it to shorthand some of the community development featured in the other papers (more on this in chapter 2). The *Times* stands apart from the other papers in its initial mission: while the other papers were designed to make money *as newspapers*, it seems (in both its iterations) to have been designed primarily to make money by funneling business to Burgher's general store and to his printing business. The first issue of the *Spout Springs Times* was distributed for free, for instance, and Burgher offered free advertising space to anyone willing to fill his columns, suggesting that, at least initially, he was not looking for a profit from the paper itself. When the fire forced him to relocate, however, he found himself in need of cash. To make up the deficit, he raised subscription prices and began collecting on past-due payments, a move that did not earn much initial goodwill in Clay City if Burgher's editorials responding to these critiques are any indication. Over time, Burgher moved increasingly toward a more traditional model of the newspaper as a business in itself, charging for advertisements and regularizing subscription prices in relation to other local weeklies. He remained the editor of the *Times*—and the owner of the store—until his retirement in 1914. In 1915, his replacement, M. P. O'Mara, sold the paper back to Burgher. Although the reason is not explicitly given in the paper, it is easy to imagine, given Burgher's bellicose personality in his editorials, that he found O'Mara's treatment of his legacy, particularly as a Democratic booster, somewhat lacking as the partisan tone of the paper becomes much less dramatic during O'Mara's short tenure. Burgher ran and edited the paper until he retired for a second time in the 1920s, passing the paper on this time to his two children.[15]

THE *BREATHITT COUNTY NEWS*

Of the papers in my study, the *Breathitt County News* is the shortest-lived of them all, running from 1901 to 1911, with archived issues available only from 1903 to 1909. Because the first two years are not available for review, I have not had the opportunity to study the *News's initial* efforts to create a community in as much depth as I have those of the other papers. Despite the lack of issues, however, I opted to include the *News* in this study, both so that all papers that met my time and geographic criteria were included in the study and because the *News* was located in the county perhaps the most associated with the idea of Appalachia—Breathitt County, known as "Bloody Breathitt" owing to a series of killings described as a *feud* in newspapers throughout the United States. As T. R. C. Hutton illustrates, the word *feud* is "applied to various sorts of violent events in order to make their particulars less knowable." In this case: "As railroad tracks and corporate capital made their way to Breathitt County, there were plenty of exogenous sources of violence. . . . But the political nature of white intraracial ('white-on-white') conflicts was obscured by repeated references to endogenous causes: isolation from the outside world, poverty, lack education, mania for revenge, obsession with kinship and racial vestigiality (Anglo-Saxon or Celtic 'blood') in eastern Kentucky's 'feud belt.'" The result of such rhetorical obfuscation was that economic and outside development continued to be seen as a potential *solution* to feuding rather than being recognized as one of the inciting causes of violence. The political violence that occurred in the county began shortly after the Civil War, but it came to head in the 1890s and the first decade of the twentieth century with multiple murders, including those of some county officials. These acts of violence were aimed at alternatively gaining and breaking political control of the county, which was run by Democrats but featured a strong and committed Republican faction.[16]

Into this environment stepped J. Wise Hagin, a county judge. Hagin was himself a Democrat, but he was part of an 1899 split in the local party over support of William Goebel or his primary opponent, John Y. Brown, in the election for governor. This division resulted in the development of a series of fusion tickets, in which dissident Democrats in the county joined with Republicans to overcome the local party machine, led by James Hargis. In 1901, Hagin founded the *Breathitt County News*, not as a moneymaking enterprise directly, but as part of the effort to unseat the party machine in favor of the fusion party. The paper, then, occupies a strange political position, one in which most candidates endorsed are Republican despite its stated identity as a Democratic paper. Hagin's paper features militant political diatribes similar to those found in the *Mountain Advocate* and the *Clay City Times*, but these are directed against two groups. First and foremost, Hagin often takes the Hargis faction to task, albeit at times indirectly. Notably, this puts the paper directly at odds and into conversation with the *Hazel Green Herald*, which was located in neighboring Wolfe County and wholeheartedly supported Hargis's faction. Second, Hagin takes to task reporters and newspapers who represent the violence in Breathitt County as representative of a lack of civilization in the region and calls attention to the political issues underlying the violence. Despite its political intentions, it is important not to underplay the paper's economic motivations: by breaking up the Hargis faction, Hagin would improve his own economic prospects and improve his chances of holding public office; similarly, Hagin embraced the business as a moneymaker, touting his supposedly superior abilities as a printer frequently in the paper to drum up business. He appears to have closed down the paper as its initial raison d'être became less necessary; as the Hargis faction started to lose power in the face of threats of prosecution, having an organ through which to promote fusion tickets became less necessary and presumably less profitable.[17]

Table 1. Number of Issues Reviewed	
Paper	Issues Reviewed
Big Sandy News	436
Hazel Green Herald	311
Mountain Advocate	229
Sprout Spring Times/ Clay City Times	504
Breathitt County News	82

Newspapers as Archive

Each community, then, had its own unique flavor and set of interests. Each editor brought particular and idiosyncratic motivations to the work of producing the news. Yet, despite these differences and their often-curmudgeonly relationships with one another across the divides of business and politics, the editors nevertheless engaged a community of readers that stretched across the mountains and often overlapped. References to other newspapers in the study as well as many newspapers that are no longer extant are near constant. Taken together, the newspapers illustrate a vibrant literacy scene throughout the period of my study, one that reached into nearly every county we now think of as central Appalachia.

Through their frequent descriptions of schooling, the newspapers demonstrate a widespread commitment to education throughout the region. The presence of correspondents from towns and villages throughout central Appalachia speaks to the reach of the newspapers, the widespread nature of literacy in the area, and the correspondents' abilities as both readers and writers. In their role as sponsors of literacy, the editors act to "enable, support, teach, model, as well as recruit, regulate, suppress, or withhold literacy," and, while they do so for their own advantage, as Brandt suggests, these acts are ultimately to our advantage because they allow us to recover the everyday uses of literacy in communities of the past and consider how those uses affect current perceptions and possibilities for Appalachians.[18]

2

Sponsoring Literacy in Appalachia

When we think about sponsors of literacy in Appalachia, a number of groups with missionary-like aspirations come to mind: the founders of the Hindman and Pine Mountain settlement schools, for instance, who were northern women "called" to make a difference in the mountains and funded largely by Protestant organizations. We might also think of the teachers who made their way to coal and lumber camps, also typically northern women who were inspired by depictions of poor, illiterate children in the press. In later years, we might think of the VISTA workers brought to the region by Lyndon Johnson's War on Poverty. In each case, the structure of sponsorship is imagined as a highly literate outsider selflessly giving up the comforts of home to come to a benighted region where few people read or wrote, delivering to it the light of literacy.[1]

Part of the reason for the predominance of these images is that there is little archival evidence to refute the image of an illiterate populace, for reasons discussed in the introduction. Yet, even when researchers have access to rich depictions of literacy relationships and sponsorship practices in Appalachian communities, we are often treated to an analysis of those texts that show Appalachians as "willfully ignorant and cognitively and culturally unevolved" because, as Kim Donehower explains, these interpretations often take as their starting point existing views of Appalachia—views that present illiteracy as the norm rather than the exception. When we start our research by looking for lack, we very often find it. If, instead, we begin with the assumption that literacy was the norm, evidence abounds to support this case.[2]

By turning to the local newspaper, we turn to a text that in its very existence belies the myths so often associated with the region. Such texts reveal that a powerful and reciprocal literacy sponsorship existed throughout the region between editors and the readers of local papers. These men set out to cultivate communities of readers not from altruistic goals but as a way to support their own economic success. In doing so, they leave behind a record of highly literate community members who actively lobbied for their preferences and enforced them on the editors, making clear that these readers were not only engaged with texts but also critical, agentive readers capable of articulating their desires and imposing their will. In short, the newspapers make clear that the most frequent and perhaps most important sponsors of literacy in the mountains were not the outsiders who imagined themselves as literacy saviors but the men who negotiated sponsorship relationships with their communities on a weekly basis.

Michael Schudson points out that, as we examine the history of newspapers, we need to be wary of relying on a discourse of need—"if it exists, and people use it, it must have come into existence because people felt a need that it served"—as we analyze the reading publics that newspapers serve. In this study of newspapers in the region, it is certainly tempting to make the case that because these five newspapers existed in the interior counties of Appalachia—four of them for very lengthy periods—there was clearly a fully formed reading public that needed a weekly newspaper. The newspapers themselves, however, demonstrate that each editor set out to create a reading public for his product rather than the reverse. To build a subscriber base and advertising clientele, the editors found it necessary to make the case for their papers in their early issues, selling their concept to a seemingly skeptical public. Once the papers were established as viable, the editors continued to take on the role of sponsors of literacy as a way to cultivate a community of readers willing to pay for the pleasure of the news.[3]

In the case of each of the newspapers I study, there appears to be no local call for a new newspaper. For instance, the editor of the *Hazel Green Herald,* Spencer Cooper, appears to have moved to Hazel Green specifically to begin a paper, not because he was familiar with the community in any way, but because he saw a potential business opportunity in the area's lack of news representation. As Schudson suggests, for Cooper as for other editors "the news media serve the needs not only of readers but of the entrepreneurs who produce the news institutions." As George Payne explained contemporaneously, newspapers of the era drew their income from advertising dollars rather than subscription prices. As he puts it: "The matter of circulation was, in a great majority of instances, important only as it enabled the newspapers to command advertisements." J. E. Burgher, the founder and editor of the *Spout Springs Times* and the *Clay City Times,* was such a dedicated businessman that contemporaries "speculated that [his] quest for mercantile business was his sole reason for starting the paper," owing to his frequent advertisements for his general store in his early issues. For J. Wise Hagin, the founder of the *Breathitt County News,* the paper seems to have been a tool meant to forward his unique and potentially dangerous political views in the area known as Bloody Breathitt. The *Mountain Advocate*'s hometown, Barbourville, had already seen the failure of several papers when Daniel Clark began his weekly, so there was actually negative evidence that the community was in need of a paper. In these cases, the editors who began these newspapers did so as an entrepreneurial project whose success was not guaranteed by community desire or enthusiasm.[4]

As such, the newspaper editors became, in many ways, sponsors of literacy as a way to create the enthusiastic reading public needed to support these business endeavors. Each editor set out deliberately to describe and model appropriate reading practices and leaned into the literacy myth, encouraging his readers to see a subscription to the news as a path to social standing, moral improvement, and economic success. More important, each editor sought to create a community of readers, a sense that being a member of the reading public made one a better member of the local community. As we have seen, Benedict Anderson describes an imagined community as one in which most members "will never know most of their fellow-members, meet them, or even hear of them, yet in the minds of each lives the image of their communion." To create this kind of community among a highly dispersed population, the newspapers modeled an image of readers and reading in which subscribers could share—through which, to use Anderson's term, they could commune. Sandra Gabriele and Paul Moore detail one example of this kind of community creation through newspapers; in their study of the weekend editions of several Canadian newspapers, they argue that nineteenth-century editors "drew upon public knowledge of the idea of an American Sunday paper" as a model for their own papers, "craft[ing] a community" of subscribers, and drawing on a preexisting knowledge of newsprint to "mak[e] the 'weekend paper' in general a cultural form." I argue that, by framing their weekly newspapers in relation to a series of other texts and, quite explicitly, in relation to their ideal readers, the editors of the newspapers in this study participated in a community-crafting process similar to the one Gabriele and Moore describe. This process employed a variety of techniques, including explicit appeals for subscribers and negative critiques of nonparticipants, instruction in appropriate reading practices both for the newspapers themselves and for other texts in the community; and guidance on selecting reading materials.[5]

Cultivating a Community

To begin the process of building a readership, the editors often made explicit appeals to local citizens, presenting a case for why the paper was important and urging readers to subscribe and advertisers to enroll. The *Herald* provides an example in its first issue: "**The Herald** is the only paper published in Wolfe county, and circulates largely in the counties of Wolfe, Morgan, Powell, Menifee, Magoffin, Breathitt, Elliott, Estill, and Floyd, the latter seven being without a newspaper of any kind. THE HERALD is, therefore, **The Best Advertising Medium in Eastern Kentucky**, and advertisers can reach more people by an advertisement in its columns than by any other means. Try it, and be convinced." Here, Cooper communicates very directly to potential sources of income, presenting his paper as a tool to enrich their businesses. Obliquely, he is also making an appeal to readers: if they want to know what's for sale, this is the best place to look. In a place of far-flung communities where travel to a general store could be a day's commitment, knowing in advance what stores had a particular good in stock and at a reasonable price was a significant piece of information, one that might well be worth the cost of a subscription.[6]

The *Mountain Advocate* made its appeal on a more personal level, describing its "first subscriber": "Before we left Georgetown, Ky., for this city, our mother placed in our hand a silver dollar, and as she did so, remarked, 'I want to be the first to subscribe for your paper, and I want to establish the precedent which I hope you will follow,—to always collect in advance.' God bless that dear woman. . . . Now who will follow the example she has set?" Alongside this touching description of the editors' mother appears a panegyric to the town of Barbourville, demonstrating that the editors have embraced their new home and seek to celebrate it through the paper. Concerned, perhaps, about being perceived as outsiders, the editors demonstrate that supporting the paper will be a form of supporting the town because the paper's goal is to uplift the town. They also tap into the universal pathos of the mother/child separation, essentially urging readers to make their mother's vision of their success a reality.[7]

The *Clay City Times* also fills its early issues with explicit celebrations of its town, and Burgher, the editor, carefully structures these to show that supporting the paper is itself a form of support for the town. He begins by encouraging readers to support local businesses in general terms: "Sell all you can and buy all you can. If you have the means invest in something that will give employment to somebody. If a rich man starts a project, encourage him. If a poor man starts a project, help him." He then makes his appeal even more explicit. "Don't be afraid," he writes, "to thrust your hand in your pocket to help a public enterprise." By thrusting their hands into their pockets to support the newspaper, Burgher suggests, the subscribers are not only helping a local businessman but also performing a thoughtful community service. Cooper, the Clark brothers, and J. E. Burgher, then, each make an appeal to an imagined readership. While Cooper imagines his readership primarily in terms of economic relationships and the Clarks and Burgher in terms of community relationships, all invite readers explicitly to imagine themselves as part of the reading public their papers will embody.[8]

As the papers become more firmly established in the community, the editors' relationship with the imagined community changes somewhat. Each editor continues to preach the importance of the local paper; the *Big Sandy News*, for example, features a typical column declaring that the newspaper's "patrons reap far more benefits from its pages than its publishers, and in calling for the support of the community in which it is published it asks for no more than in all fairness belongs to it." However, each also begins to speak more directly to those who do not demonstrate wholehearted support of the enterprise. Rather than appealing to the good nature and community spirit of readers to encourage subscriptions, the editors instead frame those who refuse to subscribe (or pay for their existing subscriptions) as antagonistic to the larger community of readers they have formed. They ask their readers to join them in condemning those who do not embrace the project of the paper and frankly insult and threaten those who are perceived as unsupportive. Conley, of the *Big Sandy News*, illustrates this approach well in his dismissal of those who unsubscribe out of anger at his editorial choices, likening his paper to the Bible of the community:

> After you get angry and stop your paper, just poke your finger in the water, pull it out and look for the hole. Then you will know how sadly you are missed. A man who thinks a paper cannot survive without his support ought to go off and stay awhile. When he comes back half his friends will not know he was gone, and the other half will not care a cent, while the world at large kept no account of his movements. You will find things you cannot endorse in every paper. Even the Bible is rather plain and hits some hard licks. If you get mad and burn your Bible the hundreds of presses will still go on printing

> it, and [if] you stop your paper and call the editor names the paper will still be published, and what is more—you'll read it on the sly.

Conley shows a great deal of self-importance in comparing the act of stopping the paper to the act of burning the Bible, a sacrilegious suggestion in a deeply faithful region. In issuing this comparison, he illustrates his belief that his other readers—those who aren't stopping the paper—consider its contents of such importance that they, too, will share in his condemnation of those who would forgo the paper out of pique. His statements show a firm belief in the power of his imagined community; were his paper less well established as a community fixture, such a column could well have led to further angry readers. Instead, he appears convinced that his words will serve to rally the community around him.[9]

Conley takes a similarly negative tack in his frequent reminders to readers that it is a crime and that persons can be arrested for collecting a newspaper by mail and then refusing to pay for it. In later issues, he goes further, humorously likening refusal to pay for the newspaper to a sin, writing that the "Lord wasted mud when he made a man who would take his county paper for 5 or 6 years and never pay a cent." The *Hazel Green Herald* similarly insults those who refuse to pay up, declaring: "Of all the sneaks that ever scandalized a newspaper subscription list, the meanest is the one who, after reading the paper for a year or more, tries to beat the publisher by saying he subscribed for only six months."[10]

In a particularly morbid example of this kind of dunning for subscription money from the *Clay City Times,* Burgher includes a syndicated column that describes the graves of various kinds of foolish people in the town: "a man who blew the muzzle of a gun to see if it was loaded . . . the girl who tried to start a fire with kerosene . . . a boy who tried to jump on a moving train . . . the man who stood in front of a mowing machine to oil a sickle." All these, the article suggests, "sleep on undisturbed." Only two men linger in a state of disarray: "Over in the potter's field may be seen the bleaching bones of the man who tried to whip the editor, while [only] a short distance away rots another carcass which even the buzzards refuse to touch—the man who got his home paper on credit and refused to pay for it." While one hopes that Burgher did not actually believe that those who failed to pay were doomed to eternal damnation—although the overall tone of the paper leaves the matter in some doubt—clearly the column is meant to communicate to readers that nothing could be more foolish or uncouth than refusing to pay one's subscription. All readers would recognize the characters described, and all would recognize and disdain the ignorance that led to the deaths mentioned; these were everyday hazards of life at the time that all children were taught to avoid. The insult here is not just that the nonpayer is a thief but that he is an idiot, even more foolish than those who have committed these fatal faux pas. In a community in which personal reputation counted for a great deal, Burgher here links failure to pay with a lack of intelligence, suggesting that the community should view such people as the dumbest of the dumb—a linkage that most readers would have sought to avoid.[11]

Against these negative depictions, the editors also offer much commentary regarding the benefits of the local news. Cooper, for instance, prints a syndicated column from the *Warsaw Independent* suggesting: "The boy or girl who is a regular newspaper reader will grow up in intelligence, and will use good language." Newspaper reading will allow these children to become "useful and intelligent citizens." The *Clay City Times* likewise appeals to the benefits for children, encouraging fathers of wayward boys to "read the newspapers to them; discuss any interesting happenings of the day, and note discussion, especially of the world's doing, in the daily papers." The *Breathitt County News* pointedly notes that the local newspaper is used as a school textbook in some areas of the country, demonstrating its value for learning. Other newspapers take a less direct approach, sharing commentary (supposedly) from readers far and wide complimenting the newspapers' contributions to the community. The *Mountain Advocate* in particular prints many comments applauding it. The second issue notes: "Scores of persons have said to us that 'the first issue was far above their expectations, and that it was the best paper ever published in the mountains.'" The *Clay City Times* takes a similar tack, featuring commentary from the *Powell County News* that averred that "the TIMES will do much toward keeping Clay City's name prominent in the business world." In each case, the editors are highlighting the role of the newspaper in improving the community, whether by offering encouragement to its future citizens by helping children learn or by supporting the town via encouraging stories and building connections among far-flung communities. By calling attention to these benefits, they imply that to neglect to subscribe is to miss out on all these contributions or, worse, to be seen as somehow not in support of these clear and important benefits to one's friends and neighbors.[12]

The editors also very explicitly implicate readers in the success or failure of the enterprise, making clear the compact between sponsor and public. The

Clay City Times engages in this most explicitly, warning subscribers early in its run that, unless outstanding bills are paid, it will not be able to recover its losses from the fire that destroyed its previous iteration, the *Spout Spring Times*, and will therefore be forced to close. Framing the issue more positively in another article, the editor, Burgher, explains that, with community support, the newspaper can be made even better, noting: "As soon as we get 300 new and paid up subscribers, we will enlarge the paper to a six column, all home set and print, and let the subscription price remain the same. Thus the enlargement and betterment of the paper lies within the power of the people." The early years of the *Mountain Advocate* and the *Hazel Green Herald* see similar references to the ability of the owners to expand and improve the paper with increased subscriptions and likewise to the threat of closure if subscribers do not pay for the news in a timely fashion. The imagined community, then, is a mutually supportive enterprise: the paper supports the town, and the town must return that favor by supporting the paper.[13]

When the editors imagined who would be supporting the newspaper, it is clear that they envision that nearly all community members would be engaged with the paper. They explicitly address many audiences. Businessmen, for instance, are exhorted to purchase advertisements in the paper, and men are urged to vote for one candidate over another very frequently, either by the editors themselves or by local correspondents (more on this in chapter 3). Women are also explicitly addressed, especially by advertisements. Magazines designed to attract women, such as the *New Ideas Women's Magazine* and the *Southern Women's Magazine*, are frequently advertised in each of the papers. Advertisements for patent medicines, which are featured in every issue, often appeal to women in their roles as mothers, framing the product as the solution to their families' woes. Given the frequency of advertisements directed at women, it is clear that the editors and the companies who chose to use the paper to promote their products understood that the imagined community built by the paper would include both male and female readers.

Some of the newspapers make efforts to cross the color line as well. While there appear to be few efforts to address the immigrant communities that were increasing in the mountains thanks to burgeoning coal camps, African Americans are often addressed as part of the imagined audience in the *Big Sandy News* and the *Mountain Advocate*. The *Big Sandy News*, for instance, frequently publishes announcements that teacher examinations—tests taken to earn a teaching certificate—are soon to be held for African

American candidates. The editor also takes what seems to be a tongue-in-cheek stab at locals who were complaining that African American populations were increasing and draining local educational resources when he writes: "In several counties in Kentucky there are no negro schools, for the reason that there are no negroes to attend. In Johnson, Letcher, and Martin there are so few negroes that there is only one small school in the county. This is rather surprising information to many persons who believed that negroes had spread over the whole State." While this aside does not paint an encouraging picture of life for African American children in the mountains, it does stand as a notable, if subtle, rebuke to those who asserted that their school tax monies were being poorly used in supporting schools for African American children. Indeed, Conley consistently takes an interest in African American education, frequently reporting on Berea College (although not always approvingly) and on local events related to African American schools. The *Mountain Advocate* is more full throated in its courting of African American readers, often reporting on the founding of African American newspapers and the activities of local and national editors of African American weeklies. For these two papers, at least, race was not a barrier to joining the imagined community of readers and writers. The *Clay City Times*, on the other hand, was an unabashedly racist paper that openly applauded lynchings of African Americans. Clearly, African Americans were not the intended audience for the paper, and the editor assumes that his racial views will help build rather than hinder the creation of imagined community around the paper. The *Breathitt County News* and the *Hazel Green Herald* only rarely discuss race in explicit terms. This may be due to demographics—Breathitt and Wolfe Counties had fewer African American residents than did the other counties in this survey. It may also be due to politics: as Democratic papers in this era, the *News* and the *Herald* were tied implicitly to violently antiblack policies. It would not have been in their political interest to court an African American readership openly. However, neither did they embrace the Democratic position on race explicitly, as the *Clay City Times* did. Perhaps, by simply staying mum, they hoped to attract as wide an audience as possible.[14]

Teaching Reading

In many cases, the editors included explicit instructions for readers on proper reading practices, creating specific boundaries for this imagined community. The first page of the premier issue of the *Herald*, for instance, featured a syndicated column from the *Mt. Sterling Sentinel-Democrat* (not coincidentally, the paper Cooper worked for before relocating to Hazel Green) that read: "It is not polite to look over one's shoulder when he is reading or writing." The article also included instructions on how to treat the producer of the text being read: "It is very disagreeable to the editor for a visitor to take his chair or use his pen, pencil, or paper without permission." Because the *Herald* intended to support itself in part through subscriptions, over-the-shoulder reading represented a monetary loss for the paper (since the secondhand reader might otherwise have bought the paper himself or herself). The article made this connection to business explicit: "What would a carpenter think if you were to go to his shop and take his saw, thus stopping him from work?" By framing the act of writing as a form of business and that of reading the newspaper as patronizing a business, the article implicitly deems reading without paying a kind of theft.[15]

As Cooper makes clear here, the editors are very invested in a community understanding of their role in the production of news; it is important to their ethos that they are perceived as members of the business community, that their role is seen *as work* and not as primarily a hobby or, more often, as a political ax to grind—particularly important given the explicit party connections that newspapers typically held at the time. Clark, of the *Mountain Advocate*, makes this apolitical role even more explicit; he notes that while the newspaper carries free-of-cost news of the major events of many readers' lives—their births, wedding, and deaths—those readers have expectations that the paper will deftly ignore potentially derogatory news. He continues: "[The editor] must not criticize the conduct of any man or woman who, on account of wealth, stands high in the community, no matter how they came in possession of same. Must be ready at all times to say something good about the old miser who, instead of giving $5.00 in the collection on Sunday, will drop a penny." Conley, of the *Big Sandy News*, aptly describes the bind in which editors found themselves vis-à-vis their readers:

> If [the paper] contains too much political matter, people won't have it. If the type is large it don't contain much reading matter. If we publish telegraph reports, folks say they are nothing but lies. If we omit them, we have no enterprise, or suppress them for political effect. If we have a few jokes, folks say we are nothing but rattleheads. If we omit jokes, folks say we are nothing but fossils. If we publish

> original matter, they damn us for not giving selections. If we give selections, people say we are lazy for not writing more and giving them what they have not read in another paper.

W. H. McDonald, who edited the *Mountain Advocate* in the 1910s, addresses criticism of his editorial choices head-on as well. Responding to critics who argue that the newspaper ought to print all news, no matter how negative, he shares an example of a man who had lambasted his paper for failing to print a story impugning a local ne'er-do-well but then found himself begging the editors to withhold a negative story about his own shady dealings a few months later. McDonald argues that he withheld both stories out of a sense of propriety and journalistic responsibility, not because of the pull or influence of either man. He makes clear that his discretion should be appreciated and understood as a gift to the town rather than as a point of critique. Spencer Cooper of the *Herald* offers a similar lesson, declaring to his readers: "The real mission of the country newspaper is to give the local news accurately and fearlessly, but in kindness, giving no unnecessary publicity to wrongdoing, yet sparing not fraud nor shams, recognizing good wherever found, striving to build up rather than to tear down." In these responses to reader's chagrin that certain negative news items aren't printed, the editors remind their constituents that their first and primary role is as an organ of the town itself: when individual actions represent the town in a negative light, they are more likely to withhold this information for the benefit of all as a way to improve perceptions of the town. Similarly, Conley reminds his readers that a dull newspaper is good for the town because it means that "no misfortune has befallen any one in our city."[16]

Burgher offers a more tongue-in-cheek reference to readers' critiques, emphasizing his belief in the readers' understanding and patience: "If, while perusing the TIMES, you are looking for errors, you will find them. In the first place, we are unable to keep from making them ourselves, and we have an apprentice as the case which insures plenty for this week." Conley's lament, McDonald's story, and Burgher's confession, like Cooper's more direct discussion of reading practices, encourage the audience to read and respond to the newspapers in appropriate ways. Readers are encouraged to appreciate what they receive rather than offering endless critique—that is, to trust the editor's good judgment regarding appropriate material for the paper. Conley in particular is also rejecting the claim that he is a political hack, a liar, lacking in enterprise, a rattlehead, a fossil, or lazy; the fact that such a rejection is necessary speaks to just how difficult it was for an editor to carve out a role for a newspaper within a community that is clearly somewhat suspicious of the motives of the newspaperman—but suspicious because of rather than owing to the lack of their ability to read the paper critically.[17]

Fred Burman, shortly after taking over the editorship of the *Mountain Advocate*, takes a more directly humorous approach to reminding his readers that the work of the editor is difficult and therefore should be appreciated. He writes sarcastically:

> The reason men envy an editor is because he has such an easy, carefree life. Advertisers, especially the home merchants, fairly mob him with advertising. Business men prayerfully beg him to do their job work for them and the readers of the inspired newspaper over which he presides insist that, if they are not permitted to subscribe and pay in advance, life will be one long, dreary thing after another.
>
> And what the editor deigns to do in return for these people is laughably easy. He buys about $6000 to $8000 worth of metal and paper and then walks around town imbibing information as to the lives, habits, customs, etc. of his fellow men. These he dresses in their best clothes so to speak, and presents them to the view of the fellow men and women. Then the editor makes metal soup, skims it, makes nifty little briquettes of it, sorts pi, occasionally deigns to run a press, corrects proof, mails out newspapers, soothes vexed people who have failed to get their copy, writes those uplift articles which are such a respected feature of the newspaper, writes advertisers, corrects addresses, does the immense banking business which enables the banks to show such large deposits in their quarterly statements and, with a few more playful duties, gets it all done in some ten hours a day.

Here, Burman is clearly intending to give his readers a laugh, but one at their own expense: the joke is that the readers too often fail to recognize the hard work the editor puts in and instead imagine him as a dilettante who cannot possibly need money but instead does the job for the sheer pleasure of the work and for the benefit of the town. While Burman emphasizes that he does, in fact, benefit the town, claiming that he keeps the local banks in business, readers are meant to take the point that, in spite of the fact that he works ten-hour days to satisfy his community, they do not adequately resemble the fawning crowds he describes—and, he implies, they should make more of an effort to uphold the reciprocal sponsorship between editor and township.[18]

As Conley, Burgher, Cooper, Clark, and Burman do in each of these examples, the editors present their newspapers as mediated texts: they highlight their own role in producing the papers, making clear that they have carefully chosen and vetted the material that appears in them. Like the editors of urban southern dailies of the period, who "portrayed themselves as objective professionals above grubby factionalism—as dedicated servants educating the people and guarding them against all enemies," the editors frame themselves as arbiters of quality, fairness, and economic well-being. Reading the newspaper is often positioned as an effective guard against unscrupulous and wasteful practices. Cooper, for instance, connects reading and purchasing in multiple articles instructing readers to buy only from those merchants whose ads appeared in the *Herald.* In the August 24, 1885, edition, he writes:

> Many of our subscribers will doubtless visit Mt. Sterling next Monday . . . and some of them will make purchases while there. To all such we wish to speak a few words: Go to Adam Baum or Trimble Bros. for your groceries; Hanley and Judy for your hardware. . . . Any of these parties will treat you in a first-class style, and you can buy cheaper than anywhere else. We protect our readers by taking advertisements of only first-class houses, and if our subscribers will deal with the parties we mention, they will find them just as represented. Paste this in your hat for reference.

Other similar columns direct the readers' attention to particular advertisements: "Our readers will consult their own interest by reading the advertisements of J. T. & F. Day. . . . In fact it will be money in your pocket, to consult all the advertisements and deal accordingly." In both these articles, the act of reading was depicted as a currency exchange. In the former, reading acts as a barrier against nefarious businessmen; in the latter, it explicitly produces (or maintains) money for the reader. Readers were thus taught to understand a subscription to the *Herald* as an investment that would pay off in later business exchanges.[19]

Similarly, the editors cautioned their readers regarding other kinds of promises. The *Breathitt County News,* for instance, urged its readers: "Beware of the 'something for nothing' advertisements that appear in newspapers and magazines. All of them are frauds." The message, of course, is that no such ads would appear in *this* newspaper but that the audience must use caution when reading other sources of news. Indeed, on the very same page, the editor compliments the quality of his own advertisements, writing: "You will find on the second page an ad of a sheriff's sale. We doubt if any other office in the mountains could get up such an ad, but we have a printer that can do things." The *News*, he makes clear, is the only place to buy and read important advertisements for legitimate and quality products.[20]

The newspaper editors clearly assume a literate public: they are not teaching their audience to read from scratch. Rather, their greatest fear seems to be that the purpose of the paper will be misunderstood and measured against preexisting expectations of what printed text should be. By clearly outlining what purposes the newspaper can serve, they attempt to create a community of readers bound by shared understanding and expectations. They promise economic, social, and educational benefits in exchange for the community's loyalty (in the form of a subscription payment or advertising placement). The success of these endeavors is found in the lengthy runs of all but one of the papers in this survey: clearly, the editors were able to create a community of readers ample enough to sustain their work.

A Mountain of Texts

The editors' sense of their readers as a vibrantly literate community is clear in their choice to advertise other kinds of reading material and to link the papers themselves with other reading. The papers—particularly the *Herald*—offer a number of special deals on books that include a subscription to the paper in the purchasing price. Each newspaper also carefully develops club relationships with other newspapers across the state. Such relationships allow readers to subscribe to multiple papers for a single set price. For instance, the *Clay City Times* offers club rates that pair the paper with the *Louisville Courier-Journal*, the *Cincinnati Enquirer*, and the *Louisville Commercial*, all of which were Democratic papers like the *Times*. The *Mountain Advocate* paired itself with the *Louisville Herald*, a fellow Republican paper. We can see, then, two threads of sponsorship: on the one hand, the editors hoped to tap into existing partisan affection for these other papers to gain subscribers to their own weeklies; on the other hand, they were encouraging their readers to do only a certain kind of additional reading beyond the local paper.

They were not willing to encourage readers to delve into papers that did not share their ideological leanings, even if such a relationship might have been economically beneficial by pulling in additional subscribers from the other side of the aisle.

The editors give space in the paper to advertisements for a wide variety of texts. Advertisements for joke books, religious texts, dictionaries, fictional texts, and schoolbooks appear in each paper, a mix of respectable texts that is in keeping with the kinds of book advertisements published in other late nineteenth-century newspapers and magazines. The placement of these advertisements is also significant: they are included alongside advertisements for commercial goods and services. In the September 16, 1885, edition of the *Herald*, for instance, an advertisement for *Webster's Dictionary* appears surrounded by ads for wagon repair, sign painting, schooling, and dry goods. This placement depicts an idea of reading (and purchasing) books as inseparable from the other functions of daily life. In Cooper's imagined readership, books are commodities *equally* as valuable as other goods—not less valuable because of the lack of education in the region, as is often suggested by the mythologized idea of Appalachia, and not more valuable because of the scarcity of written material. The very presence of these advertisements belies the notion that books were unobtainable in Appalachia. Though cost barriers undoubtedly influenced the number of books actually bought by eastern Kentuckians, the idea of Appalachia as an area with little access to books is rendered absurd by the sheer volume of book advertisements printed in each of the newspapers.[21]

The placement of these advertisements also tells us a great deal about outsiders' perceptions of eastern Kentucky readers. Most of the newspapers—certainly the *Big Sandy News*, the *Hazel Green Herald,* and the *Mountain Advocate*—listed themselves in newspaper directories that many nationwide companies used to direct advertising placement. Advertisers then contracted with the paper to feature particular ads on the basis of their understanding of the target audience for each newspaper. As we will see below, the editors certainly vetoed some advertisements that they felt did not foster the imagined community they desired. Most advertisements, however, seem to be accepted, and the advertisements that appear in the papers for products manufactured outside the mountain—including most books—are in place because the companies who purchased the space believed that the paper's readers constituted a healthy market for their product. Thus, the publishing houses and individual authors who placed advertisements for dictionaries, almanacs, fiction, and other reading material clearly assumed that enough interested readers existed in eastern Kentucky to justify the expense of placing the advertisements. The publishing houses also frequently placed ads to hire agents to sell books door-to-door—yet another indication that they perceived a hefty market for their goods. Readers are asked to cement this view by referencing the advertisement they've seen in the paper when they write to inquire about such placements. Other kinds of companies, such as Standard Oil, often use references to reading to encourage the public to buy their products; a patented lamp, for instance, is touted as ideal for one's library. Clearly, while the myth of an illiterate Appalachia gained an audience in the 1910s, it was not so compelling that it prevented advertisers from missing out on this moneymaking opportunity.[22]

In addition to publishers, other kinds of businesses used texts to sell their products, again illustrating their sense of the audience's affinity for reading. One notice alerts young men that they should "write at once for illustrated pamphlet free" from the Voltaic Belt Company. Another advertisement announces that the "Medical Annual, known as Hostetter's Almanac . . . may be obtained, free of cost, of druggists and general country dealers." A variety of catalogs are also offered for free. Both the editors and the advertisers imagine the papers' readers as a potential purchasing public best motivated through reading (rather than, e.g., demonstrations, which were also used throughout the region).[23]

Experienced Readers

While the advertisements for written texts certainly make clear that the area was, indeed, a mountain of texts, the editors' own discussion of reading material and reading practices makes clear that they imagined their communities not just as mindless consumers but as deeply critical readers. Brief reviews of books appear often, as do occasional reviews of those reviews. For instance, one *Herald* article remarks: "A marked spirit of deferential courtesy is shown by the more important of the English reviews in treating the works or personality of American literary men." This syndicated column suggests that readers are aware of what are the more important English reviews and of who the American literary men are and that they are apt to read reviews in the first place. It also suggests to *Herald* readers a way of understanding these reviews—to recognize that these English reviewers are likely to treat a text written by the "spurred" authors differently than they might treat a text by a less-established author. A notice on the same page encourages a similarly critical reading of the Bible: "The Bible revisers base their confidence in the ultimate general acceptance of the new version on the precedent afforded in the history of the King James version, which came into general use despite the fact that it was not received by the generation contemporaneous with its production." In a region often characterized as practicing a uniformly fundamentalist form of Christianity, this passage calls forth readers who understand the Bible as an edited text—one revised by the hands of men, past and present, rather than the unmediated word of God.[24]

The clearest examples of editors sponsoring readership in their communities is through their use of serialized stories to encourage subscriptions. Each of the newspapers, with the exception of the *Hazel Green Herald* and the *Spout Springs Times*, featured serialized stories. The *Big Sandy News* and the *Breathitt County News*, in particular, relied heavily on them, using the early pages of the newspaper to emphasize their presence tucked into the back pages of the paper—thus, the casual browser might be lured into the story and encouraged to take a subscription to complete it. This strategy was common among periodical editors in the nineteenth century. As Patricia Okker explains in her study of American serial novels: "Many nineteenth-century editors saw the magazine novel as crucial to their professional success—arguing for instance that the 'serial novel' was a 'prime necessity to the popular magazine.'" Okker argues that one of the reasons serial novels were so popular and powerful was that "one of the effects of having to put a serial novel 'down' at a particular moment is that readers experience the text together": "Best-selling novels in book form are often read in a sort of community, but readers are rarely in the same place in the text at the same moment. But that sense of community—that social experience—is precisely what happens with popular serial novels." In their continual effort to create a community of readers, the serial novels featured in the newspapers served to unite the community members around a shared textual experience; the editors likely hoped that the serial novel would become a point of conversation in the town, leading to a sense that reading the newspaper was essential to being fully a part of the local milieu, and leaving those who had not yet subscribed with the feeling of being on the outside looking in. Serial novels also served a somewhat paternalistic function by demonstrating to subscribers the kinds of novels they *should* be reading: typically, stories of love and adventure rather than more titillating stories of crime, for instance.[25]

The editors also sponsor shared reading activities by publicizing local reading clubs and literary societies. Although it is not always clear whether these societies are reading exclusively published works or also composing their own material and distributing it among themselves, in either case the correspondents who discuss these clubs and the editors who choose to include these tidbits of local meetings in the paper are certainly representing these clubs positively, tacitly encouraging additional local readers to join. Similar encouragement to read along with one's neighbors can be found in the periodic contests surrounding reading and writing activity; while these do not happen regularly, the papers do feature such contests from time to time. One example appears in the *Mountain Advocate* as the editor encourages locals to participate in a contest sponsored by the *Lexington Leader:* "Prizes amounting to $1000 in gold will be awarded to those who guess the greatest number of book titles represented by pictures." He attests that "guessing the titles of the books is great fun and everyone has a chance," indicating how common a broad literary knowledge is in this community.[26]

One of the most striking examples of the ways in which the editors worked as arbiters of appropriate reading material for the community arises in regard to an autobiographical book by Caleb Powers. In 1900, Powers was convicted of complicity in the assassination of Kentucky governor William Goebel, a highly publicized and politicized murder. One's opinion of Powers's guilt often derived from one's political beliefs, and the papers demonstrate this well. The one staunchly Republican paper in my study, the *Mountain Advocate*, posted many lengthy defenses of him in its pages, and it certainly encouraged readers to take a look at his own explanation of events in his book. The *Clay City Times*, by far the most fervently Democratic among the papers surveyed, takes the opposite approach. Burgher explains to his readers that he has been asked by the publishing company to feature an advertisement for Powers's autobiography. The text, he argues, does not accurately represent events. "Like all other murderers," he writes, Powers "doesn't tell but one side" of the story. In response to the ad request, then, he notes: "We decline the offer, as we don't care to aid in liberating murderers or their accessories, and will leave this job for others to do as their [*sic*] seems to be some anxious to continue this class of work." It is worth noting that this column features elements of Appalachian dialect ("doesn't tell but one side" being a relatively common sentence construction in the region but not elsewhere) that I have not noted in any of Burgher's other columns, as well as at least two typographic errors (including the *their/there* switch). Given the stark difference in tone, style, and care taken with this passage in relation to the rest of the newspaper, we can infer that Burgher was quite passionate and engaged with this topic and that his vehemence stems from deep personal belief rather than simple expedience. He is, of course, turning down what was likely a significant advertising outlay in order to take this stance. It was worth it to him, he makes clear, in order to ensure that his paper fostered the kind of community he wished to represent: one in which murderers—at least Republican ones—did not command the attention of the local reader. By the same token, his readers certainly held expectations of him: had he chosen to run the Powers advertisement, Democratic readers might have seen this as a violation of their sense of shared community with the paper. Publicly disavowing the advertisement allows Burgher to flaunt his commitment to his vision of the community.[27]

The editors also made it a point to steer their readers toward certain other newspapers—namely, those that espoused similar party politics—and away from others. A short note from the *Big Sandy News* is typical of this genre: "The name of the Western Argus is the most recent addition to our exchange list. This new paper . . . is a very interesting and ably edited weekly. Our wishes are for its success." By mentioning a paper that its subscribers would otherwise be unlikely to encounter (the *Argus* was based 150 miles west), the *News* editors seek to support a fellow newspaperman and also recommend a particular piece of reading material to their subscribers. This paper—rather than sheets closer to home—is the one that is worth the readers' money because it represents the *right kind* of reading material. Indeed, the *Herald* makes this statement explicitly, branding itself and certain other newspapers "The Right Kind of Reading Matter." Readers are likewise warned away from certain other papers. In a somewhat convoluted example, Milton Conley shares the insults lobbed at a fellow Democratic paper by a Republican rival, calling attention to the absurdity of the "bouquets" the Republicans are putting before the public, and, in doing so, illustrating that the Republican paper is not to be relied on for accurate news. Conley also heaps scorn on papers that contain what he considers inappropriate material. He critiques the *Louisville Courier-Journal*, for instance, writing: "The man who 'makes up' the columns of the Courier Journal must use a queer brand of O-be-joyful to cause him to put some pathetic lines on the death of a child into his 'On the Funny Bone' column." Although, like Conley's *Big Sandy News*, the *Courier-Journal* was nominally Democratic, it had offered problematic endorsements in previous presidential races, which almost certainly left Conley feeling freer to criticize his fellow Democrats for poor taste.[28]

At times, local loyalties conflicted with political beliefs, and editors found themselves walking a tightrope to balance their competing missions to support their towns—by supporting its residents—and to support their political parties. J. E. Burgher demonstrates this line in his comments on a new paper, the *Paris Globe:* "We add to our exchange list the Paris Ill. Globe and note that John T. Griffith, formerly of this place, is publisher. Mr. Griffith was connected with the Clay City Chronicle during the boom days. He is making of the Globe the same he did of the Chronicle, a very readable paper. But one objection can be found to his paper, and that is its politics. It is a Republican sheet." Here, Burgher clearly responds to local expectations that the deeds of a successful resident be reported with pride, just as the deeds of so many other locals who have moved elsewhere are noted. However, he cannot in good conscience simply recommend the paper, and he makes it a point to note that its politics are objectionable and that he is not necessarily recommending the ideas contained therein. Friendship among newspapermen also outweighs partisanship; the Democratic *Hazel Green Herald* makes it a point to recommend the *Mountain Eagle*, a Republican sheet, "with pleasure" because "our whilom friend, Spence McAfee . . . is announced as publisher." Ultimately, supporting friends and neighbors seems to outweigh partisanship, though it isn't clear whether this is due to the editors' own beliefs or because the community demanded such support for fellow townspeople. In all likelihood, both play a role: because the editors are so committed to creating a sense that the newspaper's primary purpose is to better the community, supporting its far-flung members—many of whom, the editors remind us frequently, are still subscribers—is a way to demonstrate that purpose in action.[29]

The papers also advocate very directly for a general increase in reading in the community. The *Big Sandy News* uses its platform to push for an answer to why the Louisa Library is not a more vibrant enterprise. It then publishes a response from the proprietor, who explains that, while the library is active among a small group of supporters, she "should be happy if we could reorganize the Library, have regular meetings and do some work." She encourages all interested to attend a meeting and sets a date, explaining the dues needed to join. "Books are cheap," she declares, "and no one's mind should be starved for want of good, wholesome, arousing, life-giving literature." The newspaper hammers home its support of this endeavor by including at multiple points in the issue "pointer columns" that direct the reader's attention to the librarian's editorial; by featuring these in sections of the paper that might be of more interest to the casual reader—such as reports of local visitors, births, and deaths—the editors do their best to capture the attention of every possible supporter, making clear that they not only encourage but also expect readers to support this enterprise. The editors then follow up with announcements in later issues noting each time a new batch of books arrives at the library to help ensure continued community support for the endeavor.[30]

The editors often link an increase in reading to an improved moral and ethical character, reflecting the literacy myth. The *Breathitt County News*, for instance, encourages farmers to read but emphasizes that not all reading should relate directly to agriculture. Instead, some of the farmer's reading should "should be of such a kind as to develop himself as a man, to increase his general knowledge, to broaden his view of life and give him wider sympathies." This is not just an individual benefit but a necessity for the community: "[The farmer] is also a very important factor in our economic and social life. As such, he cannot dodge the responsibility that is laid upon him." If the farmers follow this guidance and take up reading for edification, "they would not only become better famers, better citizens, and better men, but life to them would have a larger meaning, and rural communities would be the more worth living in." A particular set of readers—here, farmers—is charged with the responsibility of improving the community via its reading practices. Needless to say, since one kind of reading mentioned in this column is reading that allows farmers to keep up with the politics of the day, the newspaper represents one form of encouraged reading that would result in better citizens, better men, and better communities—a winning situation for the imagined community constituted by the newspaper.[31]

Conclusion

The presence and success of the newspapers in this study do much to deconstruct the myth of a textless Appalachia, a myth that undergirds the larger idea of Appalachia that dominates historical imaginings of the region. That so many subscribers—thousands for each paper—supported not only these newspapers but also the sheets in competition and cooperation with them indicates the importance of literate activity within the community as well as, more fundamentally, the presence of a literate public capable of understanding the material in question and a public economically well situated enough to spend disposable income to subscribe to multiple texts.

To see the papers simply as static literacy objects, however, is to overlook the role of the editors in crafting a community that valued the active practice of literacy as well as the role of the community members in building consensus around appropriate kinds of reading and reporting in the paper. Faced with a community of critical readers, the newspapermen explicitly outlined the case for their papers as a worthwhile expenditure for subscribers and a necessary investment for business advertisers, and, in doing so, they leave us with a clear sense of a public that held very specific and very lofty expectations of their reading material. Inviting their communities to work with them to create a better place to live, the editors served as sponsors of literacy, encouraging particular kinds of reading activities that they believed would improve and support the community's values. By discussing these expectations explicitly, they provide us with a sense of the points on which the community was likely to agree and the points that were likely to cause friction, helping us recover the literacy practices of these areas. These descriptions paint a picture of a community that placed high demands on the editors for the quality, accuracy, detail, and entertainment value of the publications—hardly the mountaineers unburdened by books that John Fox Jr. placed in the popular imagination. The editors responded to these community demands, not only by attempting to meet them, but also by engaging in negotiations with their communities of readers regarding what qualities of texts should be valued and how the act of reading should be imagined.

Recovering the work of these editors illustrates that sponsorship of literacy in Appalachia in the nineteenth century and the early twentieth was not solely or even primarily the work of outside reformers: the sponsors of literacy who entered the lives of many Appalachians reliably each week were men of Kentucky—Appalachian either by birth or by choice—who did not attempt to dictate the terms of literacy to the community but who worked to build coalitions of readers who would support their enterprises in exchange for high-quality textual experiences that fit community notions of appropriate literacy practices. By recovering this history of reading and sponsorship, we can reframe the historical narrative of Appalachia: we can recognize that a highly literate community engaged with many kinds of texts existed to resist efforts to paint the area as illiterate and intractable. Most important, because three of these papers—the *Big Sandy News*, the *Mountain Advocate*, and the *Clay City Times*—continue to exist today, we can trace a history of literacy practices that continue from the prosperous past to the mountains today. By recovering local newspapers as viable historical archives documenting an extensive history of literacy and civic participation, we can act to intervene in the narrative that Appalachians are victims of their own impoverished past or, more potently, that they are somehow to blame for the economic woes of the region. We can begin to ensure that the most recent intervention aimed at uplifting Appalachian communities does not act to reify problematic assumptions but, rather, builds on a long and powerful history of literacy practices that develop community partnerships and economic exchange.

3

Writing a Community

In her study of the history of writing practices in the United States, *The Rise of Writing,* Deborah Brandt notes: "While the founders [of the United States] would have been ready to foster and protect a nation of readers, it would have been difficult, for a variety of reasons, to imagine a nation of writers." Reading, the founders believed, was essential to a successful republic because a republic requires informed citizens. As Brandt puts it: "Citizens need unfettered access to the widest array of information in order to vote intelligently." Writing, on the other hand, was a less necessary skill, at least for the democratic project. The founders, that is, imagined a community in which, as Tocqueville suggests, "a newspaper can drop the same thought into a thousand minds at the same moment" but not a community in which those minds can write back.[1] The community, in other words, is imagined as a one-way street, one imagined *for* rather than *with* its members.

Reading, then, is often cast as aspirational: it supposedly helps us become better—better citizens, better neighbors, better people. In the previous chapter, we saw that the editors chose to tap into these associations with reading, linking reading the newspaper to becoming a better citizen of the local community. Writing in the public sphere has been cast more often as practical: as Brandt argues, it is more often associated with "work, vocation, avocation, and practical living." It is an economic engine, and "the writing skills of everyday people were captured largely for private enterprise, trade, and artisanship." Writers were not typically conceptualized as part of the imagined community formed around literacy even though their existence was obviously essential to such a community—their work was often invisible labor. In the idea of Appalachia, such work is often written out of the narrative: Appalachia is a land of coal miners and subsistence farmers, not a land of lawyers, newspapermen, and advertising men—it isn't a land where writing governs commerce. Writing is perhaps even more absent than reading from myth of Appalachia.[2]

The newspapers in this study provide a particularly potent opportunity to combat the image of Appalachia as a land without writers because they are rife with writers—writers who write for transactional purposes, yes, but who nevertheless gain community status via their writing. The editors certainly serve as writers who fulfill this role: part of their role in the paper, in the business community, and in the larger imagined community created by the paper is developed not through their role as editor but their role as writer for the newspapers. In addition to the editors, however, many other Appalachian writers appear in the pages of the news. Some of these voices appear in letters to the editor, a common practice then as now. More unfamiliar to us are the local correspondents who write columns for the paper detailing events in distant communities from which the editor would not otherwise have information. These local columns might appear, at first glance, to be simple catalogs of community events—births, marriages, deaths—but a closer look shows us that the community writers who fill the pages of each newspaper in this study have much more to say. Their writing serves to demonstrate that the imagined community built by the newspapers was indeed a reciprocal community, one in which the readers had a chance to speak back to the editor and to one another, publicly negotiating the norms of appropriate literate interaction. In their writing, as in that of the editor and the letter writers, we have some of the only surviving examples of everyday writers and writing in nineteenth- and early twentieth-century Appalachia—writers writing for profit but not as their primary work, writers who define themselves not *as writers* but as other kinds of workers who also happen to write. In allowing these voices to speak—or, rather, write—directly to us and hearing what they have to say, we can recover voices that have been simply written out of Appalachian history, and, perhaps, we can make the stories they bear tellable once more to a wider audience of readers.

Calling All Correspondents

Correspondent columns in the newspaper—columns detailing community events in small locales some ways distant from the paper's home—did not arise from an altruistic motive of providing a voice for local citizens. The motivation seems to have been purely economic: correspondent columns provided the material the reading audience was most interested in obtaining, and the editors were desperate for content that would appeal to communities outside the immediate town in which they resided. The *Clay City Times* makes the need for local news very apparent, the editor, Burgher, opining:

> It is a fact that many good items are lost to newspapers every day by the modesty of people who fail to tell the editor matters concerning themselves. The right thing to do is to stop a newspaper man on the street or any other place you happen to meet him, and tell him you were away on a visit; that you have relatives visiting you; that you were or had been doing good. If you have been doing anything mean, keep that to yourself, for others will tell it.

Here, Burgher is inviting readers to accost him in the street in order to find the items he needs to fill his paper! He believes that his community desires positive news items to balance out the negative ones, his final comment here making clear that he receives enough salacious news as it is. Given all the editors' references to readers' critiques that they publish negative news stories that they shouldn't, he is almost certainly correct in his assertion here that the paper will be more appealing with additional positive items of community interest.[3]

When the editors do not have news from a given community, they are not shy about seeking out writers to contribute. Spencer Cooper of the *Herald* begins calling for correspondents from the earliest days of his paper, writing, for instance: "We want a correspondent in every precinct in the counties of Wolfe, Morgan, Breathitt, Menifee, Magoffin, Powell, Elliott, Estill, Perry, and Floyd. In fact, at every point in the mountains. Write for terms to agents, &c." Other papers, particularly the *Breathitt County News* and the *Mountain Advocate,* seem to have no difficulty initially attracting correspondents but in later years must seek out additional writers. A typical column for the *Mountain Advocate* reads: "The Advocate would like to have a good lively correspondent from every postoffice in the county. News is what we want, and we will print it in our columns." If correspondents do not fulfill their role, their absence is noted. The *Herald* asks, soon after its request for correspondents: "What is the matter with our correspondents at Bothwell, Frozen, and Rousseau? We would like to have all points represented. Gentlemen, send us the news, please." This call out to missing correspondents from particular communities highlights the extent to which Cooper knows his readers expect this material. Rather than write to the men personally, he addresses them publicly to make clear to his readers that he is not omitting this news—he desires it as much as they do. By the same token, correspondence from particular communities is a selling point. The

Clay City Times, for example, crows: "Our Slade correspondent is back on the job this week. With an excellent report from Vaughan's Mill, Rosslyn, Slade, Spout Spring, and, in the near future, we hope, from Stanton too, we will be prepared to give almost a complete county roundup. Now is the time to renew your subscription." The broader the correspondent coverage, the more appealing the paper will be. Given the frequency of calls for correspondents from specific communities not yet represented in the paper, the editors are clearly aware of this appeal.[4]

To inspire people to work as correspondents for the papers, some editors, such as Fred Burman of the *Mountain Advocate,* appeal to civic-mindedness; the editor invites potential writers for the paper to "watch it grow and help it grow." Most of the papers also seem to offer some form of compensation, typically in the form of free subscriptions. Some are more stingy than others; the *Hazel Green Herald,* for instance, declares that "henceforth [correspondents] will not receive papers except for the week they have news letters," whereas the *Advocate* provides free papers each week regardless of contribution. The real compensation, however, appears to be in the form of community recognition: correspondents serve in a very tangible way as the spokespeople for their individual villages. They are often singled out by name in print and their neighbors encouraged to seek them out. The *Mountain Advocate,* for instance, presses people to provide news for a new correspondent: "John Peavely . . . will locate at Arkle and will act as correspondent for the Advocate from that section so please turn in news to him." The editors often extend their thanks and appreciation to the correspondents. A typical example is the *Clay City Times* note of thanks to the Stanton correspondent: "The editor is under many obligations to our Stanton correspondent for the nice lines he pens and adds to his items this week. We hope that every reader will carefully peruse the whole letter from Stanton together with poetical lines and oblige our correspondent as well as ourselves." The correspondent uses his role in the paper here to gain recognition for his poetry, and the editor is happy to repay his good work by pressuring the imagined community of readers to appreciate his compositions. Being a correspondent for the paper pays, not in a physical sense, but in terms of community attention and respect.[5]

In light of this attention and my discussion in the previous chapter of the editors' efforts to appeal to both male and female readers, it is worth noting that all the correspondents referred to by their actual names are men. Men, then, seem to benefit the most from the attention-getting element of the correspondent role. Becoming a correspondent made good sense for people who ran public-facing businesses; having people come into the establishment to give the news also meant more potential customers walking in the door. While it is not made explicit in the papers, I suspect that the correspondents who sign their work with their true names are businessmen looking to capitalize on free publicity, and, given the time and place, such business owners are men rather than women.

Many correspondents, however, signed their columns with a pen name, such as "Yellow Rose" and "Black Eye," and, in these cases, it is impossible to determine the gender of the writer. It is reasonable to suspect that some of these writers are women, and a few are even acknowledged as such by the editors. Sarah Pedersen has demonstrated that, in British newspapers of the same period, women frequently used pen names when publishing in newspapers, not because they needed to hide their identity as women—they often mentioned it in the column—but because they wanted the freedom to express unpopular views. The use of pen names in the eastern Kentucky newspapers, then, by both men and women speaks to another, more elemental reason that the correspondents contributed to the paper: to express their point of view. In a society in which it was difficult to have one's voice heard outside one's immediate community, the correspondent columns offered a rare opportunity, especially for women and for men with home-oriented work (such as farming) to speak to their neighbors and to a larger imagined community. This desire for a voice becomes clear when we see the editors frequently chiding correspondents to stick to the news—very often, they tend to venture out into more potentially divisive topics, giving their opinions on the news of the day rather than simply reporting it. The pen names function to provide a degree of anonymity.[6]

This anonymity might seem to conflict with the attention-based rewards of the correspondent role, but the physical realities of the region were such that the correspondents could be both well-known and relatively anonymous depending on the community one references. The correspondents were all well-known within their small communities—as indicated above, they were responsible for soliciting news to send to the paper, and readers were instructed to seek them out. However, they were not necessarily known outside that small community. As I'll discuss further in chapter 4, travel was restricted in ways difficult to imagine today; the state of the roads discouraged journeys, and, when people did travel, it was typically to the county seat, or the largest town, or even beyond, to other county seats via the railroad, rather than to other small, far-flung communities in the local area. Burgher of the *Clay City Times*, as mentioned above, brags about having correspondents from Rosslyn and Spout Springs. These communities are separated by approximately nine miles as the crow flies; via county roads today, the distance is 12.5 miles, a journey that takes about twenty minutes owing to the curvy roads. In 1919, the roads were even less direct, and the journey would still have been made by horse, by wagon, or, in some cases, on foot. Such a journey would have taken a full day of travel. So, while some people in Rosslyn undoubtedly knew some people in Spout Springs and vice versa, it was not the case that everyone knew everyone, as we so often imagine small-town life. Many residents of the two communities would not have crossed paths with one another. Thus, a correspondent in Rosslyn using a pen name could reasonably expect the residents of Spout Springs not to know who exactly was doing the writing, and this allowed a degree of freedom to express opinions that might be less than flattering to Spout Springs, such as touting the Rosslyn school as vastly superior to all others in the area, including the Spout Springs institution. Such comments are a very common occurrence in correspondent columns. Similarly, different communities in the county had at times different political leanings, and correspondents could wade—though not deeply—into the politics of the day behind a screen of relative anonymity.[7]

Negotiating the News

Although the use of pen names allowed the correspondents a degree of freedom, the editors attempted to retain control of the imagined community they were working to create via placing constraints on the correspondents. The *Mountain Advocate*'s early advice to its correspondents is representative of that offered in all the papers:

> All correspondents who write for this paper are requested to report the news briefly and confine themselves to the news. Puffs for merchants come under the head of paid locals, and would be inserted at the rate of 5 cents per line, otherwise we must pencil them.
>
> Be careful not to write anything that will prove offensive to any one; a good joke is appreciated by all, but we want to make friends and not enemies of all with whom we come in contact.

> Please read these notes and bear them in mind, and write on one side of the paper only.

While this particular example occurs near the outset of the *Advocate*'s run, similar reminders appear in all the papers throughout the period of the study. Such advice makes clear that the correspondents could function as a double-edged sword for the editors: on the one hand, their contributions were invaluable in attracting readers from many disparate communities; on the other hand, the correspondents had ample opportunity to offend as many people as they pleased. Such offenses could easily lead a miffed patron to cancel a subscription. Just as we saw in chapter 2, the editors had to be very careful to print the news without telling *too* much news—news stories that showed the community in a negative light were often shelved or toned down. Editors needed correspondents to exercise the same discretion, yet, at the same time, they needed to cater to the correspondents' desire to express themselves freely. Thus, the relationship between editors and correspondents was one of constant negotiation, much of which took place in full view of the larger reading community in the pages of the newspaper.[8]

At times, the interplay between the editor and the correspondents features instructions couched in good-natured ribbing from the editor. The *Big Sandy News,* for instance, gives a lengthy list of dos and don'ts to its correspondents that plays heavily on humor:

> The NEWS wants the news all kinds of legitimate news but we want it "hot off the wire." We also want it as briefly stated as possible. We want this week's news not last week's as our columns are not ancient history. We would rather have a five-line item as soon or before it happens than a column on the same subject next week. Again, we don't want opinions from correspondents, nor have we space for adjectives, furbelows, flowers or "taffy." . . . Bear in mind also that we don't want anything on the tariff or a last year's bird nest. We want all the news but must have it in a digestible shape. Please respect and spare the waste-paper basket.

The advice Conley provides here is much more specific than the more general advice provided by the *Mountain Advocate* or his own similar introductory pieces of advice throughout the paper. Clearly, this column responds to a series of specific offenses to appropriate writing techniques that correspondents have recently committed—namely, being too slow to submit their news and too fulsome and opinionated when they do. Conley's joke about the wastepaper basket is indeed a quip, but it is also a warning: fail to follow the rules, and you won't have your opportunity to speak. By the same token, Conley makes clear how much he relies on the correspondents: if they don't get the news in, *it doesn't appear*: it isn't as though he has other correspondents lined up to fill the gap, so he is depending on these local writers to keep his readers informed. He intends to push his correspondents to get the news in "a digestible shape," but the tone remains lighthearted because he cannot afford to push them too far.[9]

At times, Conley is even more direct to all his correspondents, opining: "Every few weeks we are compelled to admonish correspondents to write nothing but the truth, as some of them continually violate our instructions." He frames this as a problem not just for the *News* but for "[the correspondents'] neighbors, and the public." Similarly, the *Clay City Times* urges readers to come and share their news, in part to ensure the accuracy of the information received. Burgher writes: "Printing hearsay reports is often very unreliable, but generally is the only way we have of getting news to the people." "Friends" who can stop by the office and give a detailed report in person, he avers, provide much more accurate news. This is a clear dig at the correspondents, notably as Burgher is nearing the end of his run as editor, yet he is frank that he has little other option if he is going to provide a full picture of events in the county. In essence, by including this frank statement, he is putting the onus on the community rather than on himself, to ensure that the information provided in the newspaper is accurate. Conley, by the same token, makes clear to the correspondents that it is the community that is damaged by the falsities correspondents peddle, not the newspaper alone. In this reciprocal relationship, in order to be heard correspondents have the responsibility to provide relative accuracy in their reporting.[10]

When the correspondents do not hold up their end of the bargain, the editors do not hesitate to distance themselves from correspondent content publicly. Notably, however, they *never* take direct responsibility for the material printed in the correspondent columns. They are clearly in a position to control what is published in the paper; as we saw in chapter 2, they often make explicit these editorial choices. They are also, from a pragmatic standpoint, able to add material from other sources to fill the pages; indeed, they frequently make reference to having too many correspondent contributions in a given week and having to push some to the following week. Several editors also reference the many verses of poetry that are sent in to the paper; Conley references keeping these on file in case space allows for publication. The choice to publish correspondent material, then, is clearly *a choice*—but one that the editors take no responsibility for making. Instead, they paint themselves as victims of the dishonest correspondents and do everything they can to distance themselves from the material.

In a relatively lighthearted example of the genre, Burgher of the *Clay City Times* explicitly denies responsibility for the columns: "The newspaper man may be blamed for a lot of things he can't help such as using partiality in mentioning visitors, giving news about some folks and leaving out others, etc. He simply prints all the news he can find." If it is sent in to the office, then, he will print it, whether or not it is an accurate reflection of community events. At times, this distancing is much less lighthearted, and editors will deny responsibility for specific columns. In light of the complaints received against a particular correspondent, the *Big Sandy News* publishes the following: "A complaint has come in against the Horseford correspondent, using the nom de plume 'Black Eye.' It charges false statements made with the intent of injury. We have so often denounced this sort of thing in correspondents that we think it unnecessary to say more than to state that our denunciation applies to this case as well as to all others which have or may hereafter come to light." Conley here acknowledges the scope of the problem, in a sense discrediting his own paper, and all but guarantees that such a thing will happen again. Yet, despite this potential threat to community trust, he doesn't take the specific correspondent to task, instead relying on previous denunciations to do his work for him.[11]

The oddity of this statement highlights the unique role of the correspondents in the imagined community of the newspaper and the limits of editorial authority within that community. Although the editors are certainly the most powerful members of the imagined community, they do not create it alone: *all* readers and writers exercise agency in molding the norms that govern the community. Correspondents exercise this agency by flouting the conventions editors attempt to set for them, and their power within the community becomes evident when we see that editors refuse to exercise any of their seeming authority to curtail the correspondents. While fellow readers and writers will at times serve as a check on correspondents (more on this below), for the most part correspondents seem to have free rein to report the news and express their opinions as they see fit. Correspondents, then, ultimately exercise as much control over the tone of the paper and, at times, the content as the editors themselves—because the readers demand that this be the case. If editors felt that certain correspondents truly posed a threat to readership, their material would be omitted, just as other potentially offensive material is. Their lack of action makes clear that the potential readers lost because of correspondent misbehavior are far less important than the potential readers lost by a refusal to print correspondent news or even to exercise editorial control over that news. By repeatedly distancing themselves from correspondent content even as they continued to give those correspondents a voice, the editors attempt to have the best of both worlds: the local news items that readers most desired but also the continued trust of the community.

A Community of Critique

While the editors demurred from imposing restrictions or even offering particularly strong denunciations of correspondents who did not meet the expectations outlined in the newspapers, fellow correspondents and community members often step in to act as arbiters of appropriate writing behavior. In regard to correspondents who fudge the truth, it is very often members of the community who make the editor aware of these falsehoods rather than the editor discovering these on his own. A good example of this phenomenon appears in the *Big Sandy News*. A local man from the town of Hulette writes:

> The writer noticed in last week's News a letter from this place, which I am sorry to say, was one continuous lie from beginning to end. Now, I can't understand why some people are so devoid of truth as to write such infamous lies as appeared in that letter. Sauerkrout [the previous week's correspondent], you would do well to retire from your journalistic career, we think, or retire long enough to take a few lessons in the blessed truth, of which you are at present so very, very ignorant.

He then signs his true name, presumably in a rebuke to the original author's use of a pen name. A review of the column in question reveals that the accuser here, Laban Compton, is mentioned in the column; he is said to have been "calling on Miss Annie Piles [on] Sunday." While the phrase *calling on* has at times been linked to the idea of courting, in the pages of the *Big Sandy News* it seems to be used more generally to refer to any visit rather than one specifically involving a romantic connection. The intense response, then, seems out of proportion to the original offense and speaks to the importance the information carried in the columns held within the community.[12]

The editor follows this diatribe with a note: "The name signed to the letter referred to was that of a young lady and will be furnished to anyone who desires to know." This is perhaps the boldest statement Conley makes in response to the many, many instances of correspondent peccadilloes in his paper: lie to us, and I will reveal who you really are and let you be held accountable to your community for your falsehoods. Ironically, the correspondents were clearly well-known in the community as, elsewhere in the newspaper, subscribers are instructed to direct their information to their local correspondents. Thus, the threat here is largely for show: everyone involved in the transaction is well aware of who is doing the writing. What is interesting is that the accuser chooses to take issue with the correspondent in this public fashion rather than settling the disagreement privately—it is more important to right the public record and, in all likelihood, to prevent future offensive reports than it is to receive personal satisfaction for the perceived slight. The newspaper, then, becomes both the forum for a break in community norms and the forum for its repair—the negotiation takes place in full view of all readers, with the editor explicitly calling on them to hold the writer accountable by requesting her name.[13]

While Laban Compton's complaint seems to be based on the fear that his intentions toward a lady might be misunderstood, at times the issues taken up between writers to the paper are of a more serious nature. Judge J. S. Miller, for instance, writes in to the *Mountain Advocate* to disdain a correspondent's attacks from the previous week: "I desire to say in reply to the writer from Hammond, Ky., who did not have the manhood to sign his own name to his statement, but signed a false name instead, that his statements, as far as they refer to myself, are absolutely false, almost from start to finish. I do not know as to the others." Though similar to Laban Compton's diatribe, Miller's response deals with much more serious accusations as the writer, signed "Straight Rider," accuses Miller of using his elected office improperly when redistricting the Hammond area. After articulating at great length the inconveniences to voting that the new precinct locations present for each small community in the district, Straight Rider declares: "We don't think the judge has done us right, because he did not go according to the will of the people and the petition. . . . We are surely going to elect a new judge and try him. The 12th day of November [Election Day] is coming, and God send it, is the prayer of the voters in this precinct." Miller's response is, given the harshness of the accusations against him, relatively measured; still, it is a response that again attempts to use the public conversation to right the wrongs done to him by other newspaper writers. Given the reputation of eastern Kentucky in this period for exacting blood retribution for crimes against one's character, it is particularly important to note that the papers are full of examples similar to the exchanges between Miller and Straight Rider: exchanges in which offense is given and offense responded to *in print* rather than in word or deed. The imagined community fostered by the newspaper creates a space in which disputes in the physical community can be resolved peacefully, if not always amicably.[14]

Correspondents at times respond to these kinds of published critiques of their work, sometimes doubling down on their previous statements, thus rebutting their critics, and sometimes retracting them. On rare occasions, a correspondent will do both at once, as in the following example from the *Clay City Times* in which the correspondent apologizes for his statements about the school but stands by his other reporting that has occasioned comment:

> The writer sincerely regrets to think that anyone would think that he would slander our school. He is a loyal friend to it and moved to Stanton for it alone. The school has a splendid corps of teachers, as fine as we could ask for. . . . My statement was misconstrued for which I deeply regret. . . .
>
> The writer has always had sympathy for the editor of a newspaper. He expects the hatred of law breakers and to incur enmity when he takes a stand for the right. I expected to be mis-quoted, to have false statements made and accredited, to incur enmity, to be accused of referring to this one or that one, in fact to expect most anything when I commenced writing Stanton news. I always speak what I think if it is the truth and if it hurts then it must hurt; I speak plain never beating around the bush; while I want friends yet if the whole county is against me I will take my stand against lie swearing, vote selling, illegal carrying of liquor and such like.

The correspondent here responds to various accusations from the community regarding his columns. This defense is noteworthy in that he specifically cites his freedom to express unpopular opinions as his motivation for taking on this job; he is perfectly willing to sacrifice his local friends in order to create a space for himself within the imagined community of the paper. He is anxious, however, to respond to the specific critique that he has insulted the local school, which speaks to his desire to be understood—this is not simply a case of blowing off public steam (as we might see with a Facebook post today) but a concerted effort to create a proactive dialogue to improve the community. For that conversation to happen, the correspondent takes the responsibility to correct his own mistakes and take public responsibility for them.[15]

At times, the interplay between correspondents is more playful and speaks to the newspapers' ability to create interpersonal relationships across distance even as it still serves to critique appropriate writing norms. In the May 13, 1885, issue of the *Hazel Green Herald*, two correspondents call attention to the absence of a column from a frequent contributor. The Tazewell County, Virginia, correspondent Garkey writes, "Wanted to know—where is our Grassy correspondent?" while Longfellow, of Rothwell in Menifee County, writes sarcastically, "Say, you Grassy creek correspondent, what has become of you? We heard that you had purchased a sack of molasses and had been robbed, is this statement true?" In the parlance of eastern Kentucky, referring to someone or something as being "like molasses" is a reference to his or her tardiness at completing a task (i.e., to being as slow as molasses at finishing one's job). To suggest that someone has been robbed of molasses is to take the insult further, indicating that one is not fast enough to keep pace even with one's molasses (i.e., to be *slower* than molasses).[16]

Two issues later, the Grassy Creek correspondent responds to these writers, picking up on Longfellow's pun, and cleverly turning the insult to his advantage:

> Your correspondents "Garkey" from Cedar Bluff, Va., and "Longfellow," of Rothwell, Ky., seem to be very anxious to know where your Grassy creek correspondent is. I will just say to them I am "On the Wing." Longfellow wishes to know if I lost a sack of molasses. All I can say to him about that is, the ladies say I have never lost any of my sweetness from an earlier period of my existence down to the present time.

Though Garkey and Longfellow succeed in calling attention to the Grassy correspondent's failure to meet expectations, the Grassy writer responds by demonstrating his prowess with language. In all three columns, the correspondents police one another's writing practices. Indeed, these accusatory exchanges between columnists become so frequent that Cooper occasionally intervenes, imposing his own views on proper practice: "Correspondents are respectfully requested to confine themselves to furnishing news, and abstain from flings at each other." In keeping with the hands-off editorial practice regarding correspondents, however, he neither deletes these slings nor refuses to publish them. In fact, the interchanges among the correspondents seem to promote the imagined community further, giving correspondents and readers from otherwise distant locations (Tazewell County, Virginia, and Menifee County, Kentucky are about 160 miles apart) a reason to invest in *all* the information contained within the paper even when it did not directly pertain to their communities. It is fair to say that the correspondent columns are the primary vehicle for creating a sense of communion among the physically separated readers that make up the imagined community each paper calls into being, and, in this sense, we can see that writers and writing are powerful, respected forces in eastern Kentucky in the period of time during which the region is most roundly condemned as illiterate and textless.[17]

Writing to the Editor

While correspondent columns are by far the most common way for community members to have their voices and opinions heard, letters to the editor are also a common method for local writers to hold forth on the issues most important to them. Although correspondent columns and letters to the editor have much in common—both frequently express controversial opinions, and both appeal to the larger community, not just the editor, in making a case for those opinions—letters to the editor are generally one-off instances rather than extended contributions, and they generally tackle one specific issue rather than a variety of events and ideas that permeated a given community over the course of a week.

In most cases, letters to the editor take up political topics. At times, these editorials make clear just how closely eastern Kentuckians kept up with papers and opinions outside the region. One editorial writer, for instance, writes in to defend Caleb Powers, who was running for Congress: "I see that the *Evening Post*, of Louisville, a Democratic paper, is trying to jump on our man Powers. I do not know what a Democratic paper has got to do with a Republican primary anyway." The author goes on to point out that the criticism from the *Evening Post* and other Democratic papers is serving primarily to unite the Republicans behind Powers, and he follows with a ferocious defense of Powers's wealth. The letter, then, serves two purposes: the first is to convince fellow Republicans to cast their ballot for Powers; the second is to engage in the most public way possible with writers in other parts of the state (in this case, Louisville).[18]

Unsurprisingly, given the political rationale for its founding, the *Breathitt County News* is where some of the most searing interactions occur. One letter, featured as the first column on the front page of the paper, responds to several pamphlets titled "The Thousand Sticks" (which the writer characterizes as itself a newspaper, though there is no evidence of a true newspaper by that name) that have been distributed throughout the district. This letter, written by the circuit judge candidate John Eversole, dismisses thoroughly both the content of the pamphlets and the character of the writer. A sense of the tone can be gathered from the following representative passage, drawn from diatribe that takes up nearly half the front page:

> This great paper, the "Thousand Sticks," this elegantly edited paper that is being sent all over the district free, (it had to go free, you know, or not at all) has no circulation.... [U]ntil you began to send out copies free you could have thrown a rock from the press room out of its circulation. It is after me, you know.
>
> Since this race for judge has been on the voters have been getting it free. Who do you suppose pays for these copies? What you see in this great paper is Mr. Lewis [the other candidate] blowing his own horn.
>
> Oh, but this great paper comes out in one issue with a petition signed by a number of citizens of Leslie county endorsing Mr. Lewis, a kind of certificate of Republicanism, you know. How many signed it? Oh, my 74! How many voters are there in this district? More than 6,000. How many are Republicans? At least 5,000. What a showing, and that coming from a man's home county.

That Eversole decides to respond to these slings and arrows from "The Thousand Sticks" via print is in itself a rebuttal of the mystique of Bloody Breathitt, which would suggest that such insults were all but guaranteed to result in bloodshed.[19]

It is also a rebuttal of sorts of Eversole's own last name since one of the most famous feuds in eastern Kentucky—one covered by the national press—was known as the *French-Eversole feud.* Eversole and the editor, J. Wise Hagin, are both obviously aware of this metadiscourse: Hagin uses the paper on many occasions to rail against portrayals of Breathitt County in the popular press, and Eversole would certainly have been aware of the reporters from major news outlets, including the *New York Times,* seeking the real story of the Battle of Hazard, the culminating event in the French-Eversole feud. By opting to respond forcefully to these accusations in print, Eversole is—regardless of the content of his response—explicitly distancing himself from the violence that has characterized community politics in the past. That Hagin chooses to publish such a lengthy rebuttal to another "newspaper" on his front page speaks, too, to the political purpose of the *News*—which is, after all, a nominally Democratic newspaper here presenting an opportunity for a Republican candidate to defend himself. Both men are working deliberately to create an imagined community that fosters the kind of physical community both desire: a community in which the Democratic Party machine no longer controls the area but also one in which this is achieved via the force of ideas rather than at the end of a gun. Both men must also be conscious of the very real physical risks they are running in presenting such a response: while both are working to achieve the kind of society in which politics does not beget violence, they are also quite aware that this kind of political dispute has very recently resulted in assassination—yet they choose to take the risk.[20]

While Eversole's commentary against his opponent is political, print-based attacks occur for many other reasons, such as business rivalries or professional discord, but most often they are in response to supposed rumors started by one party or another. An example from the *Big Sandy News* combines these types of complaints when one correspondent avers that a local doctor has been spreading false rumors that the correspondent had a tapeworm. Following the attack, the doctor writes a letter to the editor and requests that it be published in full to rebut the claims against him:

> John T. Griffith, of Cherokee, Ky., stated in an article in your paper that I knowingly misrepresented him by telling all over the country that I expelled a tapeworm from him. I never told anyone that I expelled a tapeworm from John T. Griffith, although many seem to think he was the man. I expelled the tapeworm from a man in

> Lawrence county. He requested me not to tell the public where I got it. I took the tapeworm before I put it in alcohol and showed it to Al Burton, R. T. Berry, and a number of others at Blaine. In my opinion John T. Griffith was influenced by exaggerated misrepresentation by my rivals at Blaine which actuated him to have such request printed. If John T. Griffith had wanted that report rectified he could have more easily vindicated himself by requesting me to have published a denial.

In recounting this rather bizarre series of events, the doctor effectively recovers John T. Griffith's reputation, rebutting the tapeworm rumor. He does, however, perhaps dubious work with regard to his own reputation—he attempts to clear himself of spreading false rumors, but, in doing so, he reveals that he was not as careful as he might have been with delicate health information since he admits to demonstrating the tapeworm to "a number of others" in spite of his patient's request to keep the matter confidential. Even so, his testimonial is necessary to undo the potential damage to his reputation wrought by the original story since rumormongering is treated in the paper as an extreme breach of courtesy—a violation of the contract among readers and writers—just as we saw above in Laban Compton's ferocious response to his local correspondent. By responding in this way, the doctor not only sets straight the facts of the case but also turns the tables on Griffith in his final lines, making clear that it is Griffith who has spread false rumors about him when the issue could easily have been settled via a more civilized writing exchange mediated in the pages of the *News.*[21]

While many of the letters purportedly to the editor respond to other community writers, some do actually address the editor directly and prompt a response from him within the pages of the newspaper. In one such instance, the *Clay City Times* receives so much criticism of a particular column that Burgher does not publish the letters individually but instead posts a response to all complainants:

> We have received some letters relative to the recent examination for teachers, in which some of the writers, apparently applicants for [teaching] certificates, take us to task for stating that the applicants violated an oath when they received or gave aid during the examination. We do not know if the oath was administered or not at this examination. It is customary to do it, but it is immaterial whether

> or not it was done. The person who does receive or give aid when taking an examination of this kind is absolutely unfitted for a teacher, no matter whether they take any oath or not.

That the *Times* has received multiple letters on this subject speaks to the degree to which the column criticizing exam takers hit a nerve within the community. While Burgher does acknowledge here that he may have been incorrect about the specifics of the oath being taken, he doubles down on his overall critique of those who did not follow the spirit of the examination process. Here, we see him once again negotiating appropriate practices with his community members on the pages of the paper. While he might have left these letters unanswered, this would not have fulfilled the tacit contract he has with the community—he would seem to be dodging the question, which might lead to questions about his honesty or reliability. He might also have backed down, simply acknowledging his incorrect information, but this would allow for what he—and, he must assume, his readers—considers a violation of appropriate norms. As we shall see in the next chapter, schooling is perhaps the most important issue within the newspaper; to let this challenge to good schooling practice go unanswered would be to undermine the community's clear commitment to improving education standards. Thus, Burgher opts to thread the needle, acknowledging his mistake frankly—he doesn't know about the oath—but demanding that good schooling be paramount.[22]

Editors as Writers

Editors responding directly to their detractors are but one of many examples of them taking on the role of writer as well. While most of the material in each issue comes from other sources—the correspondents, advertisers, and articles taken from other (often larger) newspapers—the editors make key contributions to each issue *as writers*, voicing their views on important issues within the community. These contributions range from brief and innocuous commentary, responses to other newspapers, and lengthy diatribes on current events. Like the correspondents, they seem to view these columns as their opportunity to share their views with the community and shape public opinion, and they take full advantage of this opportunity while still carefully negotiating the norms of the imagined community of readers.

The tendency to take up the writer's pen regarding issues not directly related to the paper itself (excluding, of course, advice to correspondents or responses to letters to the editor) is more pronounced in the more political papers—the *Clay City Times*, the *Mountain Advocate*, and the *Breathitt County News*—than in those papers that attempt to stay above the political fray, even though not all the commentary offered speaks directly to politics. Although I have thus far presented the imagined communities created by all five papers as quite similar—as indeed they are—this marks a distinct difference, one that is established early in each paper's life and that continues throughout its run: the editors of these three weeklies have created a community in which their readers expect and apparently accept, if not welcome, their thoughts on a variety of issues. The editors do not abuse this privilege: while such editor-authored columns appear more frequently in these three papers, they are still a minor component of each paper, far outnumbered by the correspondent contributions and columns drawn from other newspapers.

In almost every case, editor-authored columns can be read under the broad heading of *defense of the town*: the editors are seeking to give credit to the town by calling out a unique or positive characteristic, rebutting claims made against the town or its citizens, or offering claims against other towns and their newspapers—claims that, by implication, suggest that their own town is much superior. At times, these defenses are backhanded, yet they are defenses nevertheless. An example of this dynamic—one that also provides a startling commentary on race relations in the United States—appears in the *Clay City Times*: "We Southerners are spoken of as being cruel to negroes and etc. and when we resent an insult from their hands our rural routes are stopped and postoffices closed and etc. True enough we string them up for certain crimes and it is also true enough that we string up whites for like perpetrations. But we have never yet dynamited a negro church like they did over at Carlisle, Ind., last week." This is a bizarre column on several levels. A constant booster for his town, Burgher frames his defense of Clay City by seeming to brag about the fact that the town lynches people of *all* colors—hardly a celebration of lawfulness and peace. Given his careful avoidance of most coverage of the violence in nearby Breathitt County, it is particularly out of character to see him acknowledging the violence that was only then, in 1905, beginning to ease. It seems that he cannot resist the opportunity here to rebut northerners who have accused southerners of racism and punished them accordingly, even if he must grant the premise that the county itself is a violent place. He seems to imagine that drawing this equivalence between extrainstitutional violence toward African Americans and extrainstitutional violence toward whites somehow paints his community as more enlightened than many of the surrounding areas—and, if the lack of response is any indication, his readers seem to buy it. To his credit, in the context of the article he is reporting on *and condemning* a crime against African American parishioners, which is unusual for the time in a Democratic paper, particularly in the South, since such attacks were instead often celebrated in print—but one wishes that his defense did not rest on such a bleak point of comparison.[23]

All the editors are keenly aware of the negative perceptions of the South and of Appalachia in particular. For Hagin of the *Breathitt County News,* this extended specifically to his county: Hagin was appalled that it was known around the country and the world specifically because of its reputation as Bloody Breathitt. In spite of that, he was also appalled at the events that led it to be called such, and, unlike the *Hazel Green Herald*, whose correspondents at times celebrated the guilty parties in the assassinations in the county, his paper made it a point to condemn such violence. A typical column from Hagin threaded this needle well. For instance, he writes:

> The deposition of Moses Feltner . . . concerning the assassinations in this county, which was published in the Lexington Herald, Lexington Leader, and the Courier-Journal last Sunday, has caused a great deal of comment throughout the State. While it was a revelation to the outside world that such things could happen in any community, many of our citizens were familiar with most of the statements therein, as they had heard them rehearsed before, although silence is considered golden in this county.

Here, Hagin is engaging in a multilayered critique of the press and of the community. His comments about the shocking events implicitly condemn them and, in particular, the fact that they have "caused a great deal of comment throughout the State"—in other words, he is offering a subtle insult to those who have brought this attention to the county. On the other hand, he is presenting the uproar as behind the times as the facts of the case have been known for quite some time (and mentioned in the *Breathitt County News*). He is also critiquing the journalistic norms here, for, while he has indeed reported on these events, he has done so minimally and with what he would likely call *good taste*; he has not sensationalized them or made them the talk of the state because "silence is . . . golden" and such things are best diminished rather than trumpeted. As we saw in chapter 2, the editors are invested in presenting their towns in the best possible light, even if that means omitting certain community events; Hagin is criticizing these big-city newspapers for not observing the same tact.[24]

Critiques of fellow editors are the most common type of editorial writing in the newspapers. One editor frequently takes another to task for how certain events have been portrayed. Burgher provides us with some insight as to the motivations behind these disagreements by describing one in the *Clay City Times:*

> The Winchester Democrat wants the businessmen of [Winchester] to purchase a page in the Jackson [Kentucky] Hustler to advertise their advantages and business in that sheet. The [Winchester] Sun-Sentinel thinks this might create jealousy with other mountain papers and work more harm than good. We don't believe it will, as no other paper in the mountains would likely dispose of a page for such a purpose, and if they would it would prove at once to the mountain people that such paper was working for the bluegrass county and not for the county where it is published. At least, this could not be done with the TIMES; too many of our good people are emigrating to the Bluegrass already to suit one who likes to see his county improve.

Here, Burgher wades into an existing newspaper feud between two papers in a neighboring county and proceeds to lob insults at both, ensuring his own part in this continuing battle. Both papers are wrong in their arguments, he argues, because neither understands the imagined communities within which eastern Kentucky papers are situated. The goal of these papers, like the *Clay City Times*, is to build up the community. Advertising for businesses that compete with those owned by locals only serves, Burgher argues, to tear down the community and perpetuate the population drain in the area. Both papers, he suggests, are misguided in believing that mountain papers exist to serve Bluegrass patrons as these businessmen and readers are simply not part of the community within which the newspapers are imagined. There are also, it must be noted, some sour grapes being expressed here—it is, after all, the Jackson newspaper in which the Winchester men are interested in advertising, not the *Clay City Times,* despite the *Times*'s closer proximity to Winchester. Certainly, part of Burgher's motivating factor here may be a version of "we don't care if we weren't invited because we wouldn't have come anyway!" Nevertheless, whatever his motivation, he is explicitly calling on community norms to defend his own editorial behavior and insult the behavior of other newspaper editors, and his rationale for doing so is to defend the community from further loss. Such an argument speaks to the powerful hold the imagined community held over both editor, editor-as-writer, and the readers of the paper.[25]

Of our five newspapers, the *Mountain Advocate* has the most arguments in print with other newspapers because of its hard-line Republican stances. When other newspapers publish material against Republican candidates in the area, the *Advocate* is quick to leap to the defense and to continue that defense across multiple issues. These exchanges often become quite heated. For example, the *Advocate* publishes an attack from the *Mountain Echo* in order to respond to it. The *Echo* editor writes:

> The Mountain Advocate . . . takes exceptions to the editor of the Mountain Echo on account of statements made regarding Dr. Hunter. Why, of course, Mr. Advocate. Didn't Hunter import you from the accursed spot called Georgetown, in which Caleb Powers has twice been sentenced by Democratic juries, and weren't you a Democrat yourself? We will willingly leave it to the people of Knox county as to whose teachings they will repudiate and not to you.

It is, perhaps, the appeal to the imagined community of the paper that most demands a response here; the *Advocate*'s relationship with that community is premised on its ardent Republicanism, so this attack on those credentials must be answered if the *Advocate* expects this challenge of "leav[ing] it to the people" to be met with support for *it.* Clark responds with a three-column editorial touting his Republican bona fides, including that he was run out of Georgetown because of his Republican views. He then, of course, turns it back to his reading public: "We are willing to allow the Knox county people, and in fact, the people of the entire district, to pass upon who is giving the true doctrine of the party." Notably, what Clark values most here is not honesty or accuracy but militancy, and he expects that his readers will value this quality most in the newspaper as well.[26]

Conclusion

In the previous chapter, I discussed how newspaper readers worked in communion with the editors to establish and enforce norms for the newspaper and the community. This relationship was not significantly different from the present-day relationship between smaller local papers and their readerships. What does differ significantly, however, is the role of writers in the creation and maintenance of the imagined community of the newspaper. Because community members were both the primary writers and the readers of the newspaper, ultimately conversations around appropriate practices were reciprocal and often fraught. The interactions among correspondents and between correspondents and the editors show us that these norms were under constant negotiation, with the community attempting to enforce its collective will on the writers and the writers pushing back to have their voices and opinions heard.

What these columns most illustrate is that the Appalachians who made up the audiences for these newspapers weren't passive consumers of text—they weren't simply decoding the printed word. Rather, they were critical, engaged readers, and, just as important, critical, engaged writers. Far from the transactional and often invisible writing practices that Brandt describes in *The Rise of Writing*, the writers of eastern Kentucky used writing publicly and often for a variety of purposes, transactional and otherwise. Given the reliance of the newspapers on correspondent contributions, it is even fair to say that these Appalachian writers had more opportunities to appear in print that was distributed widely in their community than the majority of other Americans around the turn of the century because the editors not only devoted column space to them but also actively sought out their contributions to boost the economic prospects of the papers. While we obviously do not have a record of those community members who chose not to write, the sheer volume of voices represented in the news speaks to a community in which the ability to write was seen as a commonplace and the freedom to express oneself in writing was valued highly.

Understanding Appalachian communities as spaces full of writers belies not just the myth of illiteracy but many other myths that plague the region as well. The good-natured ribbing between correspondents from Menifee County, Kentucky, and Tazewell County, Virginia, 125 miles apart, illustrates that mountain enclaves were hardly the isolated harbors so often imagined, cut off from the rest of the world. Instead, mountain writers carried on conversations with each other across vast distances via the papers, and correspondents writing in from their new homes in Texas, Oklahoma, and states further west illustrate that Appalachia was in conversation with the country writ large. Similarly, the frequency with which norms are up for grabs in the papers illustrates that the notion that Appalachia is inexorably tradition bound and unchanging does not hold water: the newspaper writers make it clear that community norms were constantly in play, policed and pushed against in a very public forum in ways that were often contentious but illustrate, too, the falsity of the conception that all disagreements in Appalachia led to violence and bloodshed. The civil discourse created by the newspapers does put the same idea into a thousand minds at the same time, as Tocqueville suggests, but that idea is one of negotiation and ideals rather than dictates and determinism.[27]

In the contest for hearts and minds that we see play out in correspondent columns, letters to the editor, and editor-authored features, the newspapers illustrate that Appalachia was, at this point, still in the making: that its residents were actively shaping the community into the place they hoped it would and could be. These representations make it all the more tragic to realize that the communities imagined by the newspapers were already under threat and that, in many ways, it would cease to be possible to imagine them in the same way after the 1920s and the full acceptance, on a national level, of the myth of Appalachia. By recovering the hopes and goals of these earlier times, we can begin to reconceive of these dreams—we can begin to see these kinds of communities, imagined and physical, as potential realities for the future of Appalachia.

4

Schooling Appalachia

As I've illustrated in previous chapters, the cornerstone of the idea of Appalachia is illiteracy: Appalachians are backward because they can't read and thus can't be properly exposed to or acculturated into broader US society. One oddity, then, regarding the idea of Appalachia as a region dominated by illiteracy is that so much of the conversation surrounding Appalachia, particularly within academe but in mainstream publications as well, has focused on schools and teachers. Three of the often-mentioned subjects within the field of Appalachian studies are educational endeavors: the Hindman Settlement School in eastern Kentucky; the Moonlight Schools, founded in eastern Kentucky; and the Highlander Folk School in East Tennessee. One of the most successful attempts to commercialize early twentieth-century Appalachia is the novel *Christy* and its 1994–1995 television adaptation; the titular character is, of course, a schoolteacher who comes to the backcountry to educate.[1]

The common thread that unites much discussion of schooling in Appalachia is the assumption of rarity: the entire rationale for creating the Hindman and the (less-studied) Pine Mountain schools, for instance, was that northern reformers believed that Appalachians were not receiving the educational opportunities they needed and deserved. To remedy the problem, pioneering female educators arrived in the mountains with the funding necessary to create boarding schools for eastern Kentucky children. This narrative continued to hold power in the later twentieth century; it is quite common to find Appalachians represented not just as unschooled but also as actively opposed to schooling. In 1971, for instance, the psychologist David Looff writes that Appalachians "place little value on verbal skills" and "dislike . . . regular schooling." Victoria Purcell-Gates illustrates the continuation of the assumption in *Other People's Words*, depicting the illiteracy of her two primary participants, Jenny and Donnie, as reflective of a larger communal disdain for school-based learning. In more recent years, we see the theme recur, though with less virulence, in *Hillbilly Elegy*, in which J. D.

Vance attributes his success in part to his mamaw's unusual—for an Appalachian—emphasis on school success.[2]

I do not intend to contradict directly the idea that modern Appalachian culture is in some way inconsonant with schooling; on the Appalachian side of my own family, I am the first family member to graduate from high school (in 2000). However, there is a tendency to write this cultural assumption backward: that is, we tend to understand this relationship with schooling as an outgrowth of a *history of* an adverse relationship with schooling, reflected in the broad statements and assumptions used to support the settlement school movement. If we examine solely information available regarding attendance at publicly supported schools in the period of this study (1885–1920), it does indeed appear that opportunities were limited and attendance low. It is not surprising that reformers who looked at these data saw an educational wasteland and made damaging assumptions about both the education levels of the population and the cultural attitudes surrounding education in the region. However, there is more to the story, and the newspapers I've examined help fill in these gaps.[3]

First, the newspapers illustrate that a private industry of schooling was extremely active in the mountains of Kentucky and that any figures that attest to educational opportunity or attendance that rely solely on public schools vastly understate the educational activity ongoing in the region. Many students who appear to be nonattending were actually students at these privately run, ad hoc schools. Second, a careful examination of the newspapers illustrates that a lack of attendance does not reflect a lack of enthusiasm. Each paper is replete with explanations for low attendance—explanations that have everything to do with the physical challenges of attendance rather than a lack of desire. Moreover, local correspondents amply demonstrate that enthusiasm for the schools ran quite high in spite of these challenges and that communities passionately supported the local schools. These examples teach us that we must take care not to confuse material barriers with cultural attitudes.

Where Schooling Happens

Our vision of rural schooling at the turn of the twentieth century tends to look very similar to the school depicted in the televised version of *Christy*: a one-room schoolhouse led by a single teacher and supported publicly—whether by the state or by a pooled effort of community members. Certainly, the newspapers in this study do contain references to just this kind of arrangement. Frequent mentions are made of the physical conditions of schoolhouses, both to bemoan poor repair and to compliment repair work. The *Big Sandy News*, for instance, laconically notes at one point: "We understand that steps have been taken by the Board of Education to begin soon the erection of a new school building." Almost a year later it announces: "Our school trustees called a meeting . . . and levied a tax of 25 cents on the hundred dollars for the purposes of repairing our public schoolhouse." These are quite representative of frequent and unremarkable reports on the upkeep of school buildings—unremarkable, that is, in the sense that the correspondents feel no need to remark on the need for such work, taxes, or expenditures. Instead, they assume public agreement and understanding and do not elaborate. Since Kentucky education laws at the time created a situation in which, as William Ellis notes, "most county district buildings continued to be built directly from local sources and maintained by parents and concerned citizens," such an assumed agreement can be read as a widespread support for education rather than simply an inescapable result of taxation. In other words, the fact that the newspapers' writers do not feel the need to make a case for these expenditures on the physical location of schooling is worth noting, particularly in light of the space devoted to other kinds of school expenditures, such as teachers' salaries, on which agreement was far less widespread (more on this below).[4]

More striking are the columns dedicated to lamenting the condition of schoolhouses. One such indictment appears in the *Big Sandy News,* with the editors averring that the city of Louisa has "never had [a schoolhouse]" because the current facilities in which classes are held do not warrant the name owing to their poor conditions. The editors demand that the community "invest a small amount of their surplus wealth" in remedying the situation. One community writer in the *Clay City Times* asserts that the Spout Spring schoolhouse is in "imminent danger of falling down" and excoriates the superintendent for "not doing anything in assisting us to get a sufficient building." The column is so effective that the superintendent himself responds in the following issue, explaining his supposed dereliction of duty:

> I trust you will bear in mind that there are sixty-two school houses to look after in this county, and since I took charge of the Superintendent's office, there have only been sixteen days—since the first of July—that I could properly do anything toward assisting the people

> in securing better school houses, and I assure you that I have been making good use of that time. It is true I have been visiting districts where I actually knew the conditions and needs of the same, intending, after I had finished these, to learn the condition of others. I think that the trustees of Spout Springs should have notified me of the condition of their school house so I could have inspected it. I assure you I am for good school houses.

Apart from the apparently time-honored tradition of a public official trying to blame problems on an outgoing administration, the tone here makes a shared set of values clear. The superintendent does not make an appeal to a lack of funds or even to higher priorities than repairing schoolhouses. Instead, he responds resoundingly at an attack on his stewardship of the physical space of schooling, reasserting his belief in the value of "good school houses," and making clear that fixing this schoolhouse is simply a matter of time rather than a disagreement on the importance or value of such facilities.[5]

In spite of this commitment, the papers make clear that physical conditions were a serious impediment to learning. Correspondents often report that schools are idled in winter owing to a lack of heat. In a typical example, a *Big Sandy News* correspondent reports that "our school is at a standstill on account of having no fuel," while the *Clay City Times* mentions that "the Waltersville school . . . closed down before Christmas on account of having no coal." The *Mountain Advocate* reports the opposite problem, declaring that the 25 percent attendance on the first day of school is the result of the heat; students "will not start during the extremely hot weather." While we can see these problems as the result of an unwillingness to appropriate funds for the schoolhouses, nevertheless the lack of attendance is not reflective of a lack of desire on the part of students and parents.[6]

The conditions of the roads were an even bigger problem; the editor of the *Clay City Times*, for instance, insists that the "important thing is to keep [students] going until the school term closes next spring" but acknowledges that "of course this will be impossible with some of the pupils of the Waltersville school, owing to some obstacles of the road to travel in wintertime." Conditions were so bad, in fact, that the *Times* launched a diatribe against state officials who wanted to lengthen the school term. The editor writes: "We are ready and willing to pay taxes and do our bit in any way for the betterment of our schools but we certainly oppose a longer term unless the children get the benefit of the school. The last month was so cold that very few children attempted to go." Further, the *Times* argues that, while expenditures on education are important, the tax money collected for schools via a new levy "had far better be spent on good roads"—after all, if children couldn't get *to* the school, the amount of money spent on the school itself held little relevance. Debate did arise, then, on whether funds should be spent on schools. However, even these debates kept the value of education at the forefront; the difference of opinion was not whether education was a worthy endeavor but instead how best to accomplish the most good for the most students.[7]

Perhaps most important, physical distance proved the greatest hindrance to school attendance. One erstwhile community, Torchlight, bragged that it had financed its own private school district, which amply demonstrates the district's belief in the value of education, but the rationale for doing so calls attention to the problems of public schooling as well as the stereotypes that likely contributed to those problems: "The people here are not in the least backward about their wants and needs being made known in an educational way. They have organized a fine school here and employed a splendid teacher and school opened last Monday. We cannot send our children two and three miles over these rugged hills. So we have organized a school of our own by paying for it." The defensiveness in the first sentence here suggests that, unsurprisingly, the community was quite aware of how it was represented in the northern press and by reformers, such as those who raised money for settlement schools. The term *backward* draws directly from the northern press, where such descriptions of Appalachia were common. The Torchlight correspondent highlights what that narrative gets wrong: children were absent from school because of literally insurmountable obstacles, not because their parents lacked the interest or the will to send them. Taking a three-mile hike through the woods of eastern Kentucky today, it is easy to see the parents' point. Because the state was not willing (or able?) to invest in a school for the community, the community demonstrated its commitment to education by financing both the building and the teacher's salary privately, testifying to a level of commitment to education that rivals any in the United States.[8]

The Problem with Attendance

The efforts of the Torchlight community to create educational opportunities for its children offer a counternarrative to widespread assumptions that

Appalachian communities were uninterested in schooling. These narratives, both past and present, grow largely from school census data, often reported to the state by school superintendents in order to show how much funding was needed for each school year. These data show a marked lack of school attendance and render invisible the efforts of communities like Torchlight. To take but one example, the state superintendent's annual report in 1917 declared: "One of the most discouraging features of the report is that . . . less than one-half of the children attend school, at least in the common schools of the State." Modern commentators agree; William Ellis, in his *History of Education in Kentucky,* asserts: "Whereas 37.4 percent of eligible students attended school in 1860, only 36.3 percent attended in 1900, indicating nearly a total disregard of the compulsory attendance law of 1896." These statistics held quite steady throughout the period of my review and for each community served by the newspapers; there was little significant gain in attendance figures from 1885 to 1920.[9]

The closing caveat in the superintendent's report, however, suggests that these figures do not tell the whole story. The common schools in eastern Kentucky did indeed report low attendance. The *Clay City Times,* for instance, writes that the local school census showed that, of all "Powell County school children between the ages of 6 and 20 years," only "48 percent attend school." Ellis's figures reflect similar levels of attendance at publicly supported schools. Yet, as the newspapers make clear, many communities did set up their own schools, which were not included in the school census figure and are almost entirely absent from the historical record. Students attending such schools were identified in local and state records as nonattending, despite the fact that these private schools appear to have run concurrently with the common schools, offering an education of comparable quality. Ironically, then, a community's determination to provide the best possible educational opportunities for its children had the unintended effect of handing ammunition to outsiders who perceived the region as illiterate and unschooled by creating a population of students who appeared to resist educational outreach from the state.[10]

While the Torchlight community seems to have opened its own free school via community funding, this appears to have been the exception rather than the rule. Most private schools were run as subscription schools; parents (or the students themselves) would pay a set price per month or per session for the right to attend. The teacher appears to have been responsible for securing a locale for the school, thus relieving the community of the need to invest in the upkeep of a dedicated school building. In all schools in Kentucky, students were responsible for providing their own materials and textbooks, so this requirement served as no additional hurdle for subscription schools to overcome. Indeed, on the basis of the data published each year in the state superintendent's report on per capita education expenditures and the published prices of subscription schools, it appears that most teachers in subscription schools had more funds at their disposal than did teachers in neighboring public schools.

Subscription schools are referenced in every paper and throughout the time period of my study. These schools rarely occasion comment beyond the announcement of their beginning and ending and an assessment of their quality—that is, there's nothing noted as remarkable or unusual about the formation of such a school. For instance, the *Breathitt County News* nonchalantly notes: "The subscription school in Flat, which is being taught by Lloyd Lutes, is progressing nicely." In some cases, the same schoolteachers would use the periods during which common schools were out of session to run their own private subscription schools; the *Big Sandy News* notes that one teacher's "school closed on the 14th" and that "all present enjoyed a good time": "He opened a subscription school at this place on the 23rd with fair prospects of a good school." While in some cases we can assume some overlap between students attending public schools and those attending subscription schools, in other cases the change in locale of the school makes clear that the audiences for such schools were at least somewhat different and that some students who could not make the journey to the public schoolhouse were able to attend subscription schools. In addition, some subscription schools ran concurrently with the public schools and engaged in active competition with the public schools for students (more on this below), so it is clear in these cases that the two types of schools are serving distinct student populations—one of which is, again, invisible to those who examine school attendance figures in Appalachia.[11]

Commentators in all papers clearly consider subscription schools to be on a par with public common schools, and subscription school teachers seem to have taken pains to demonstrate their accomplishments, holding end-of-term demonstrations of knowledge just as public common schools did. In addition, more direct comparisons were offered between subscription schools and public schools; one subscription school teacher, for instance, "challenged the Clay City Graded School and the Stanton school for a competitive examination in the studies of grammar and arithmetic." At times, the challenges go the other way, with public schools challenging all comers; one school, for instance, "comes to the front with a challenge to any school in the county for a reading contest among the first year pupils." Following its founding—and the contest with the subscription school, the results of which are not reported—it appears that the Clay City Graded School had a difficult time enrolling students; advertisements are placed by the principal clarifying the benefits of attending the school and, subtly, calling into question the education received in subscription schools. He writes, for instance: "We strive to obtain thoroughness, however, rather than a smattering of knowledge of many things; to be deep, rather than broad. We shall undertake no patent process by which it is supposed that untutored boys and girls may be put into a cramming machine and speedily turned out well educated young men and women." The very fact that the principal needs to run such an advertisement is counterintuitive to those of us who have grown up with the US public education system and on the surface would seem to suggest a lack of interest in education; however, when we realize that the school is actively competing with other possible options in the community and that the principal needs to make a case for his own methodology against the pedagogies employed by the subscription schools, this defense speaks to the level of approval that subscription schools enjoyed within the community.[12]

While we lack sufficient archival data with which to assess the quality of education at subscription schools, the newspapers in this survey make clear that much of the data used to develop and perpetuate the idea of eastern Kentuckians specifically, and Appalachians more generally, as uninterested in education is significantly flawed. Because such assessments relied on data regarding public schooling, they fail to account for the often ad hoc nature of education in the mountains. Perhaps more important, they misrepresent the desires of parents in the region. While the traditional narrative has held that parents were unwilling to send their children to school, the Torchlight community's self-starting school and subscription-based schools show that they were willing to invest significant time and money to further their children's education.

As the newspaper accounts make clear, students did struggle to attend school on a regular basis, but these struggles were due to factors beyond their control. While today a journey of several miles to school poses no hurdle even in Appalachia, travel over mountainous terrain, particularly in inclement weather, presented a nearly impossible obstacle for many Appalachian families. Certainly, we can point fingers at a failure to invest in good roads—an issue taken up with regularity in all the newspapers—but, given the sheer volume of schools supported in each county (sixty-two in Powell County alone, as we have seen the superintendent remind *Clay City Times* readers), it is difficult to argue that Appalachian counties could afford to support additional schooling opportunities for smaller, isolated communities and individual families. The idea of Appalachia as culturally opposed to education, then, is rendered absurd by the picture provided by the local newspapers. Moving forward, we must not only reject that damaging historical assumption but also carefully work to separate concrete reality—many Appalachian children were unable to attend school—from assumed psychological motivations, instead recognizing the material conditions that played a decisive role in the development of education in Appalachia.

Politics

While the newspapers illustrate amply that more children in Appalachia received an education than has been widely recognized, they do little to attest to the quality of the education received. Descriptions of the public school system illustrate that education was undermined by politics at nearly every turn. Indeed, the problems with the public schools make clear that parents had reasons beyond geography to prefer subscription schools for their children. It is important to note, however, that the political systems affecting education in the mountains were in place throughout the state and that Bluegrass communities suffered similar struggles with politics influencing education. Nevertheless, the newspapers reveal the deep problems that county-based education systems wrought on educational opportunity.

There are, of course, some bright spots. Correspondents applaud teachers who, in their view, are doing particularly good work in the classroom. A typical example in the *Hazel Green Herald* reads: "Jim Perkins is giving entire satisfaction as a teacher at the Mize school house." A lengthier praise in the *Clay City Times* reads: "Henderson Conlee closed a most successful school at Vaughn's Mill last week. Patrons of this school tell us he has taught the best school in their district taught there for years and they say they want him for their teacher again next year." But this notice that the community desires to keep the teacher served a purpose beyond simple praise. Teacher assignments were highly politicized; both which teachers would be given a contract for a particular term and the schools to which they would be assigned were determined by local trustees, all of whom were elected, and many of whom were less than perfectly altruistic in their work. Statements in the paper regarding the desire for a particular teacher, then, served two purposes: they both notified the trustees that the community would support a particular person for the position and served as insurance against a trustee's effort to malign a current teacher in order to place his own pick in the spot the following term.[13]

Competition among districts was fierce owing to the trustee system and the conditions of the area more generally. Both correspondents and editors frequently lament the loss of popular teachers over issues of pay; J. E. Burgher, the editor of the *Clay City Times*, writes, for instance: "Miss Mayme Groves, who was elected teacher in the primary room of the city school, has resigned that position and accepted the first assistant's place in the graded school at Warsaw with an increased salary. Miss Mayme holds a State teacher's certificate and is a very fine teacher." Editors and correspondents alike seem to have recognized that the pay offered teachers left little chance of keeping a quality teacher for any length of time, particularly in more isolated communities where living conditions were less desirable (a problem rural schools continue to face today). The *Big Sandy News* makes this sentiment explicit by asserting: "If Kentucky is to have technically educated teachers . . . employment which provides something more than starvation wages for six months in the year and idleness for the other six [must] be provided for them. The best way to command good teachers is to pay them living salaries."[14]

A much later column written by the president of the Louisville Commercial Club—a club located in the largest city in Kentucky and one quite distant from the mountains—emphasizes that the problem is one that puts the mountains at a significant disadvantage in terms of teacher quality: "The cities and large towns and wealthier portions of the counties have their pick of the teachers because they pay higher salaries and the environment generally is more attractive. Thus the back districts in the counties . . . are compelled to get along with the cheapest and poorest teachers." The *Mountain Advocate* echoes this assertion: "Better teachers will come when better pay is assured." The newspapers are unanimous in their support for increased teacher pay throughout the review period, but the frequency and consistency with which the issue is explicitly raised is a clear indication that not all readers were in agreement: here, unlike for the school buildings, a case needed to be made to justify the expenditure, and each of the editors embraces the role of advocate, with the three newspapers whose towns are particularly focused on schooling—the *Big Sandy News*, the *Mountain Advocate*, and the *Hazel Green Herald*—leading the charge. In the meantime, cutthroat competition to keep the few quality teachers in the area played out on the pages of the newspapers, with communities heaping praise on good teachers to incentivize both the teachers themselves to stay and the trustees to keep them in place.[15]

Reports of fraud resulted from the low pay teachers received. The *Big Sandy News* explains such a scheme to its readers: "Some teachers . . . take up a school, usually in a rural district, and teach about three months. Then they leave that school and go to another where they can teach a full term, thus getting to teach from eight to nine months [as opposed to the usual six]. The first school is left in the middle of the term without a teacher." Despite the low pay, stories of fraud committed in obtaining a teaching certificate are also common. Because teaching certificates were awarded on the basis of a statewide exam offered periodically throughout the year, opportunities for cheating were frequent. The *Big Sandy News* highlights a specific example: "G. S. Thomas and R. S. Clark were detected in the use of copies of the questions furnished by the Superintendent of Public Instruction for teachers' examinations. Clark was arrested at Mt. Vernon, but the other man escaped." In chapter 3, we saw an example of the *Clay City Times* standing against more insidious fraud—the sharing of answers—during the teacher's exam. The *Big Sandy News* shares an article from the *Louisville Courier-Journal* that highlights the result of such efforts: "[Teachers] get their appointments by favor or fraud. . . . We permit an incompetent applicant [for a teaching position] to minister to the minds of our children upon a mere examination before Trustees equally illiterate." Here, the *Courier-Journal* is explicitly blaming the trustee system for the poor perception of education and literacy in Appalachia (and, by extension, Kentucky): the "illiterate" trustees are not solving the education problem but, rather, perpetuating both the perception and the reality of illiteracy by placing their own pocketbooks ahead of the needs of the students.[16]

Efforts were made to improve the education system of the state throughout the period of my study. The *Clay City Times*, for instance, shares an article from the *Paris (KY) Gazette* that describes the efforts of the Kentucky Educational Association to eliminate the trustee system. The *Gazette*, to put it mildly, does not approve:

> The Kentucky Educational Association at a meeting in Louisville adopted resolutions recommending radical and dangerous changes in the school law of the state. . . . The law they recommend would be an outrage upon each school district. It denies each school district the right to elect its own trustees, to employ its own teachers, and denies the district the right to buy its own furniture, fixtures, and etc., and centralizes the whole power in the hands of a paid county board that can employ teachers whether they are satisfactory or not. We believe the patrons of each school district are the best judges of their needs and wants. . . . We do not know it, and have no evidence to prove it, but it is our opinion that the big publishers of school books . . . are behind this scheme.

This particular effort by the state education association was unsuccessful, as would be many future attempts to wrest control of education from elected trustees. The editors are largely silent on this issue, at least in terms of explicit commentary; the *Times*'s sharing of this vitriolic article is the most intense statement on the issue I have found in any of the newspapers. As with many other topics, the editors here had to walk a fine line. As we shall see below, the editors appear to be clearly against the current system, often highlighting its shortcomings with particular stories of interest involving the inadequacies of the teacher-selection process. However, the elected trustees were men of great clout in the community. Moreover, the schools were important patrons of the papers, with the districts buying space in many of them to publish school-related stories. Taking an explicit stance on this issue might have fractured the imagined communities of the papers, splitting the readers between those supporting and those opposing reform. By simply sharing the evidence of the need for a change rather than explicitly commenting on it, the editors provide ammunition to those pushing for new laws while maintaining a veneer of impartiality on the subject.[17]

The newspapers make clear that instruction suffered when teachers embarked on such efforts to earn more money, with children and communities the victims of a political war waged primarily in the state capitol building. Some correspondents were quite frank about the low quality of schools resulting from such fraud. One writes in the *Big Sandy News:* "Our public school is doing no good, as school is under the control of two teachers not agreeing. . . . We think our school will be of no benefit to the students this year." Notably, in the same column, the correspondent sings the praises of the teacher at the local subscription school. That many parents opted for the subscription schools is hardly surprising in light of the political turmoil regarding teacher appointments; many subscription schools, it appears, were run by well-known teachers year after year, offering a level of consistency often unavailable in the public schools.[18]

Trustees playing favorites resulted in many serious issues, including, at times, physical violence, and the newspapers detail many of these events. The *Big Sandy News* gives the following account of a particularly large debacle (note that the shared surname of teacher and trustee are a strong indication of nepotism):

> Two of the recognized trustees [of District 55], Steven Trout and Brack Layne, employed Prof. David Layne as teacher, and on the morning of the 28th said trustees went to the schoolhouse and placed Prof. Layne in charge of the school. In a very short time after the school had opened one Geo. Deskins, another trustee, followed by two others claimed to be trustees and many others, numbering near twenty-five persons, including Miss Maude May, who was the teacher employed by the Deskins crowd, came to the schoolhouse and entered the school building, and said Deskins pounced upon Prof. Layne and they fought with their fists for many minutes. During the fracas Henry Varney assaulted and knocked to the floor, senseless, Trustee Steven Trout, and Uncle Lewis Deskins, father of Geo. Deskins, hit Brack Layne, another trustee, in the head three times with a heavy walking cane, and chased him out of the house and off the school ground. As soon as Mr. Trout regained consciousness he was forthwith pulled out of the house and marched off the grounds with Prof. David Layne, this leaving the Deskins crowd in possession of the school and they proceeded to install as teacher, Miss May.

This outbreak of violence was an extreme instance, but similar politics were at play in every teaching appointment. Interestingly, this incident is not met with particular disdain by the correspondent reporting. I would argue that this account of the violence tends to favor the aggressors, the Deskins/May crowd; while it is quite precise, it is not represented in horrified or shocked terms. This lack of disapproval is not out of keeping with other comments on the teacher-appointment process. Residents looked at that process with a jaundiced eye; in the weeks before the trustees made their selections, one correspondent sarcastically comments that "schoolteachers, locusts, and potato bugs are about to take the country," with each teacher pleading a case (and likely offering favors) to trustees for a job. Here, again, the editors allow the correspondents to voice community opinion without a great deal of additional editorial comment, and the correspondents' views are mixed: some do not particularly approve of the process, but neither do they seem to be clamoring for an alternative solution that would involve a loss of local control. Others do call for a change in the system: one correspondent to the *Big Sandy News* suggests that "it would be best to do away with the Common School System" because of the infighting and resultant poor teaching. "In this way," he writes, "it is a curse to the people."[19]

Given this environment, it is hardly surprising that many parents avoided the public school system entirely, preferring instead to pay for subscription schools taught by well-known and presumably (at least) equally qualified teachers. We have no evidence to determine the quality of education received in the subscription schools, but we have ample evidence to suggest that the quality of education received in the public schools was quite low. While this doesn't paint a particularly encouraging picture of literacy in Appalachia, it should be noted that the trustee system was in place across the state of Kentucky that and similar cases of fraud can be found in other areas of the state. In other words, the problem is one endemic to the system chosen by the state rather than to the cultural or geographic area of Appalachia. Furthermore, the newspapers illustrate once again that we cannot rely simply on public school attendance data to tell a story of educational attainment—in this case because there is little guarantee that children taught by a fraudulent political appointee learned more in school than they would have had they stayed at home. Rather, we should attend carefully to what archival research can tell us about students' achievements and the value communities placed on literacy and literacy-based activities.

Community Support

The extreme politicization of the teacher-appointment system seems to have done little to dampen community enthusiasm when it came to supporting education. Articles appear throughout each of the newspapers that laud particular schools and teachers, as referenced above. As mentioned in chapters 1 and 2, the editors of the newspapers had a clear motivation for supporting schooling—after all, the creation of a future reading public was essential to the long-term solvency of the newspaper business. In some cases, this support is very direct; the *Big Sandy News*, for instance, "kindly consented to give a column . . . free to its patrons who are interested in arousing a greater interest in our country schools." This gift, of course, represents sponsorship on many levels. While the editor, M. P. Conley, was undoubtedly committed to education, support for the schools had many benefits for him in terms of his economic prospects. He ran a stationary store that sold schoolbooks, which he spends much column space advertising, and creating a literate young populace improved his prospects for a long-term readership. The column was also likely to provide an increase in subscriptions in the short term; the county superintendent, in Conley's free column space, declares that it is "hoped that all such patrons, who are not patrons, will become patrons." Beyond this direct exhortation, it is clear, based on the near constant references to schooling in the *Big Sandy News*, that school news sells and that increasing the volume of school news is a reasonable strategy for increasing subscriptions.[20]

Not surprisingly, given this economic impetus, Conley frequently includes articles in the *News* that make an economic argument in favor of supporting local schools. He shares an opinion piece from the Louisville Commercial Club that argues: "Before we [Kentucky] can make the needed and desired progress we must get the viewpoint that it is not only our high and holy duty, but most profitable, to see our children and their schools from the investment side and provide generously the financial aid that is imperatively needed." In this formulation, investment in the school system is returned in a literal sense, with interest, in the form of increased economic activity across the state. The editor of the *Clay City Times*, J. E. Burgher, shares a similar economic argument, one in which the average salary of an "educated man" is compared to that of an "uneducated" man, with the finding that the educated man will earn $22,000 more in his working life; this, the article asserts, means that the value of an hour at school is equivalent to what a child can earn working at a lumber mill. Burgher later extends this economic argument to college attendance, writing: "A college education of the right kind and in the care of the right person is capital invested and well invested."[21]

While parents in the community appear to have been largely united in supporting education in the lower grades, students tended to leave school prior to high school; in fact, many of the communities did not have a high school until the turn of the century, and many students did indeed go to work at the lumber mill at ages when their urban contemporaries were still attending school. When high schools did appear, it was difficult for them to attract students; parents often felt that secondary education was unnecessary for the kinds of labor they expected children to engage in (agriculture or skilled trades, most often), and many families needed those children at home or at work to help support the family economically. Thus, Conley and Burgher respond to this economically based reluctance to allow further education, offering a concrete case for the monetary value of the education students received in the higher grades. Burgher also tries to argue for consolidated schools as a solution to the problem. "[The] small school," he argues, "can never afford the pleasure and exhilaration which large numbers of children of the same school age can give. The big consolidated schools are particularly strong in this hold on their older students." Here, the editors seem to be deliberately shaping public opinion rather than simply responding to it, attempting to improve support for higher learning. This, too, is inseparable from the men's own economic interests; Conley sold textbooks and other print materials to the local normal college, while Burgher was part of a local effort to open a college in his area. Again, however, the editors are careful to frame this support in terms that do not pose a threat to the existing trustee system, keeping within the bounds of the imagined communities they have constituted.[22]

In spite of the need for care in their discussions, each of the editors defends the need and benefit of education forcefully and, at times, poetically. Spencer Cooper of the *Hazel Green Herald*, for instance, argues that, as the second richest state in the South, Kentucky has plenty of money with which to fund education; it becomes a question, he posits, of what we want our souls to be. He asks: "What is the character of this strange business that men call education? It has to do with the mind and the soul and the body. It has to do with the formation of habit, with the shaping of character, with the creation of ideals. . . . What should be the character of the place where this sacred work is carried on? Within, shall it be a hovel or a home? A place of beauty or a place of ugliness?" Here, Cooper calls for increased investment in the school buildings themselves, arguing that the environment in which learning takes place shows children the value that society places on the education they receive there. Similarly, the *Breathitt County News* describes education as the sculpting of the soul: "The man has a liberal education who has been so trained in youth that his body is the ready servant of his will and does with ease and pleasure all the work that as a mechanism it is capable of; whose intellect is a clear, cold, logical engine, with all its parts of equal strength and in smooth working order, ready, like a steam engine, to be turned to any kind of work and spin the gossamers as well as forge the anchors of the mind." Burgher extends this argument further, asserting that we must "educate them, not in order that they may keep from work, or make much money but in order that they may be better prepared for the useful work of life and for the enjoyment of the lives that God has given them."[23]

To some extent, the editors are playing on the literacy myth discussed by Harvey Graff. Graff explains that "value to the community, self- and socioeconomic worth, mobility, access to information and knowledge, rationality, morality, and orderliness are among the many qualities linked to literacy for individuals." In their soaring rhetoric supporting education, the editors are explicitly identifying schooling and, by extension, literacy with economic success and morality. Improving oneself via education is a duty not only to oneself but also to the community and to God. The editors are sponsoring this model, not just because they (presumably) believe it, but as part of a larger effort to make the community a more literate and thus more productive place—a community more likely to be able to support a print-based endeavor or, as in the case of Conley, a stationary store. Other articles in the newspapers, as we've seen in chapter 2, emphasize the need for community development, and schooling is seen as foundational to that end. By sponsoring a view of literacy as a common moral good, the editors provide further impetus for their readers to pursue education for themselves and their children. They build their imagined communities around the idea that education is an essential community good and that all community members should support it. The correspondents' willingness to echo these commitments in their own columns speaks to the degree to which this was a shared value within both the physical and the imagined communities.[24]

The particular imagery used to evoke the literacy myth, however, speaks to more community-specific anxieties. While the community firmly supported the schools (more on this below), there was a great deal of cultural anxiety surrounding the potential decline of tradition; with the arrival of the extract industry in the region, more and more children were abandoning traditional agricultural occupations for work in mills and mines. Moreover, the city called: then as now, it was not unusual for young people to leave the mountains in search of opportunity, a trend demonstrated in the newspapers by correspondent columns from far-flung areas of the country (e.g.,

Kansas, Arkansas, and Oklahoma) and subscriptions to the papers received from sons and daughters far from home. The references the editors make to "any kind of work" and the "useful work of life" seek to assuage concerns that receiving an education, particularly a high school or college education, would lead children away from the community. This description responds to the concern that children who were educated might see work at home as less satisfactory by emphasizing the physical and mental benefits of education. Education, the editors reminds us, is not just the learning of new knowledge but the expansion of the self, and its role is not to push the student away from society but to encourage him or her to contribute more fully within it.

While the sponsor role that editors played in the community almost guarantees their support for the school system, the newspapers illustrate a widespread community support for and involvement in educational enterprises, from common school to college, as well. Notably, the vast majority of positive references to schooling are written not by the editors but by local correspondents. Given the relatively limited space in which to share community happenings and, as desired, opine on issues of the day, correspondents choose to devote time in almost every instance to school happenings in the community. The most ubiquitous of these is the simple status report; the phrase *the school is progressing nicely* is far and away the most common one to appear in each of the newspapers. The programs of school events are provided in great detail, and many correspondents applaud particular students for successes, providing, for example, lists of those with perfect attendance (quite similar to a modern local weekly).

Correspondents and editors alike share instances of events designed to support the schools financially. Just as we might see in a local paper today, bake sales, box suppers, and ice cream socials were common and, according to the correspondents, highly successful methods of raising money for the schools. School events are frequently mentioned and routinely hailed as well attended. A typical example from the *Big Sandy News* announces: "[A] spelling match at our school Monday night was well attended. All report a nice time." Performances and recitations at the schools were frequent, and full schedules, including the names of performing students, are included in correspondent columns. This enthusiasm extended to local academies and colleges as well. Three of the five communities in my study were home to institutions of higher learning, and all three feature reports of frequent, well-attended gatherings held in support of the institutions. The *Hazel Green Herald* and the *Mountain Advocate* dedicated specific weekly columns to events at the local academies and colleges. The *Mountain Advocate*, in fact, dedicates three such columns—two to local colleges and one to the local preparatory academy.[25]

The newspapers are equally supportive of adult education initiatives. After 1911, each paper features discussions of local Moonlight Schools, a program of night schools led by local teachers and designed to educate adults with few or no existing literacy or numeracy skills. The newspaper editors and correspondents offer consistent applause for these efforts, and, moreover, the community is often mentioned as supporting the Moonlight Schools in more concrete fashion by donating time, space, and materials to the effort. Successes are hailed, though, notably, not by name—general statistics on literacy achievements are presented, but no individuals are singled out (as was often the case in newspapers in other areas). The newspapers are likewise generally supportive of the efforts of settlement schools in the region; the Hindman Settlement School in particular receives compliments on its founding, and efforts to rebuild it after a fire are chronicled with applause.[26]

Parents also donate material and time to the public schools. One teacher illustrates the willingness of the community to support literacy by supplying books for students. He writes: "At the beginning of the term, I thought I would do well if I succeeded in building a library of 25 [books], but to my surprise we have 104 in our library and a promise of 10 more making a total of 114." The library was built using money raised by local subscription drives, pie nights, a reading circle with a membership fee, and community book donations (the fact that the community had books to donate also speaks to its commitment to literacy). Community members pitch in to repair schoolhouses, fences, desks, lawns, and steps, all dutifully reported by local correspondents eager to demonstrate to the surrounding areas that their school enjoys just as much support as any other. This, again, is perhaps the greatest testament to the importance of the school within the community: when given free rein regarding the events to be shared, nearly every correspondent opts to spend at least part of his or her column on the school and its happenings. Representing the school well was seen as representing the community well, and there is clearly a degree of competition in representing one's community as the most supportive of education and its schools as the most successful. Such reports, too, are part of the expectation held for correspondents; a correspondent who does not provide news of a school stands out from the group.[27]

The school, then, far from being an unappealing institution, served as the center of these Appalachian communities. In fact, the areas around Louisa (*Big Sandy News*), Hazel Green, and Barbourville (*Mountain Advocate*) seem to have defined themselves in terms of the education institutions residing there. Both editors and correspondents frequently expressed the belief that the success of the local colleges and academies determined how outsiders would perceive the community: as the colleges went, so went the communities. Similarly, as we see in the rabid defense of Powell County schools described above, correspondents and editors alike saw the public schools not just as a source of local improvement but as a way to represent themselves positively in relation to outsiders. In other words, each paper illustrates an underlying recognition of the negative press surrounding the area and its illiteracy and backwardness and also a consciousness that the schools themselves can serve as an effective rebuttal to those narratives.

Conclusion

It would appear that this effort to rebut the idea of Appalachia by fostering a vibrant school system was largely unsuccessful. Three of the five papers were active for years prior to the turn of the century, yet Katherine Petit and Mary Stone, the founders of the Hindman Settlement School, still cited the lack of "educational opportunity [and] the lack of community cooperation" as the rationale for founding the Hindman Settlement School. While I do not mean to suggest that Petit and Stone were incorrect—the story of the Torchlight community illustrates that many communities would have benefited from a self-supporting education institution—it is telling that Petit and Stone's narrative tapped into the widespread assumptions of the time and that no one outside the mountains seems to have questioned the need for or value of such an institution. The image of eastern Kentucky held by outsiders was not one of thriving colleges and enthusiastically supported public schools, as the editors had hoped; instead, it was of uneducated, unlettered children in need of rescue and rehabilitation. It is up to us to question to what extent the persistent belief in this image undermined the more positive realities of education in eastern Kentucky. After all, if the region is known for its poor education, why would students want to pay to attend a college there when other, equally effective options were located in the Bluegrass region? Why would students attend an academy in Hazel Green, where the townsfolk were assumed to be floundering in illiteracy, rather than one located elsewhere? Why should the state school officials funnel more money into these "pauper counties" that cannot afford to support their own myriad public facilities if the students and parents are so uninterested in education? While the idea of Appalachia was certainly not single-handedly responsible for the demise of academies and colleges in small mountain towns or for the sinking quality of Appalachian education more generally throughout the twentieth century, these narratives did play a role in undermining what the newspapers demonstrate was a vibrant educational environment that devoted time, resources, and enthusiasm to supporting student achievement.[28]

Recovering this history of eastern Kentucky and Appalachia more generally can help rewrite both the past and the future of Appalachia. The idea of Appalachia is a narrative that colors not only outsiders' perceptions of Appalachians but also, as Erica Locklear has argued, "how Appalachians conceive of themselves," circumscribing what residents imagine as possible and probable in their educational futures. If the region has always been illiterate, poor, and backward, it is impossible to imagine how the future can be different; as Harari puts it, we "take this reality for granted, thinking it is natural, inevitable, and immutable." If, instead, we recognize that the educational inequalities that now characterize Appalachia are of relatively short duration and that the region has in fact never been illiterate, poor, and backward, we can "shake ourselves free, and envision alternative futures."[29]

Conclusion

In the preceding pages, I examine newspapers published from 1885 to 1920 to demonstrate that Appalachia was not, as contemporary and present-day commentators have suggested, an illiterate, textless wasteland but, rather, a vibrant community of readers and writers who negotiated the terms of literacy and schooling in their communities via the newspaper. While any gain in historical knowledge obviously holds value and I do not mean to denigrate the study of history in and for itself, I anticipate the question of what difference this makes. While it might be an interesting historical footnote, why is it important to know that Appalachians formed such a community at the turn of the century, and what difference can such a history make in the ongoing crises of economic opportunity, environmental degradation, and substance abuse that currently face the region? Does the history recounted here have any impact as we confront these problems?

In this conclusion, I outline how our understanding—or, rather, our lack of understanding—of historical Appalachia determines our perceptions of the region in the present. Our understanding of how and when these crises came into being influences our perceptions of their causes. In turn, when we propose solutions to current issues, we do so in relation to our beliefs about these causes as well as in relation to our beliefs about the success or failure of previous attempts to solve the region's problems. Providing a new understanding of the region's history, then, can provide a new way to think about its future and about potential solutions to the very real issues of poverty and environment that face the region. To return again to Yuval Noah Harari's words, we study history "to understand that our present situation is neither natural nor inevitable, and that we consequently have many more possibilities before us than we imagine." When we take the stories that have been handed down to us regarding illiteracy in Appalachia as just that—stories—we can "shake ourselves free, and envision alternative futures." We do this, in part, by articulating new stories that more accurately reflect our past and provide us with a better sense of the possibilities available to us in the present. My findings in this text, then, represent one small step toward a more accurate understanding of Appalachia's history and a more positive sense of its future opportunities. Given the strength of the idea of Appalachia, combating these stereotypes must be part of any first steps toward reimagining what Appalachia is and can be.[1]

Cycles

Perhaps no term is more associated with Appalachian illiteracy and poverty—two concepts that are imagined as entirely connected—than *cycle*. Victoria Purcell-Gates subtitles her study of the urban, illiterate Appalachians Jenny and Donny "The Cycle of Low Literacy." In their analysis of nineteenth-century literacy, Lee Soltow and Edward Stevens describe the "vicious cycle of illiteracy, immobility, and lack of economic opportunity" characterizing the region. One of the most celebrated recent works featuring eastern Kentucky as a setting is Robert Schenkkan's 1992 Pulitzer Prize–winning series of plays *The Kentucky Cycle*, which traces a cycle of violence and impoverishment that engulfs two families over a two-hundred-year period. Articles commemorating the anniversary of the War on Poverty frequently adopt the term; even as *USA Today* describes a woman who "moved up and out of poverty" in eastern Kentucky, it is lamented that "the cycle wasn't broken" because the woman's daughter remains on food stamps.[2]

The idea of a cycle of poverty and illiteracy is, of course, not unique to Appalachia—it is a well-researched economic concept frequently applied to other minority groups. I focus here on its use to describe Appalachian illiteracy and poverty because the idea of a cycle is, in its essence, the idea that our history in some way predetermines what we are: what our parents have done determines what we will do, what our grandparents did determined what our parents did, and so forth. As the *USA Today* example makes clear, the immediate conditions of one's life—whether, say, one grew up in an economically stable household, as was the case for the daughter described in the article—are less important than the historical conditions of one's family: even though the mother had not been living in poverty at any point in the daughter's lifetime, the fact that the mother grew up in an impoverished Appalachian household was enough to doom the child to a lifetime of government dependency and impoverishment.

The psychological damage that such a model presents is likely obvious, but it is worth articulating. According to this formulation, any people who have at some point been impoverished and/or deemed illiterate have trapped their children in an unbreakable pattern *even if they themselves have managed to break that pattern.* Success—however it is measured—doesn't matter because it is our history that determines the end point for future generations. Since in Appalachia there are very few families that have never been poor, very few people who have not at some point lost their land or their jobs because of the vicissitudes of the extract industry, and very few people who have no relatives who missed out on schooling opportunities, such logic seems to doom the entire region. According to this narrative, Appalachians are hopeless, and, even if they accomplish the task of breaking the cycle, they will eventually be pulled back in. To outsiders, they have no credible stories of their past that might indicate halcyon days before such a cycle existed and, therefore, no way to frame a possible escape from that cycle rhetorically.

Among the qualities often attributed to Appalachians is fatalism—in other words, Appalachians are often imagined as seeing no way out of their situation and taking little action to prevent an unpleasant future. Even if this were true, we can certainly see that Appalachians are not alone in that fatalism—it was and is shared by those who make a performance out of studying the area and attempting to improve it. Researchers and commentators then and today, in their adherence to the idea of cyclic illiteracy and poverty, tell a story that offers no hope for Appalachians to rise above the worst circumstances of their ancestors. If Appalachians take an attitude of fatalism, then, it can be seen as acquiescing to the stories outsiders have told about the region since the 1880s, stories that have been hammered home in fiction, in the popular press, on television, and in the movie theater—stories that inescapably color how Appalachians perceive their lives and their potential.[3]

The stories that make up the idea of Appalachia are *tellable* stories. Drawing on the folklorists Amy Shuman and Ann Ferrell in her study of present-day Appalachian students, Sara Webb-Sunderhaus has explored the ways in which these students carefully consider what stories about their experiences are tellable—that is, which of their stories will be welcomed or perceived as truthful given the assumptions made about Appalachia (both by outsiders and by the students themselves). Webb-Sunderhaus's lens can, I argue, be applied even more broadly to our understanding of how Appalachia is conceived and perceived outside academe, both historically and in the present. As Amy Shuman explains: "Storyability (what gets told) and tellability (who can tell it to whom) are constrained by how experience is categorized." "Narratives," she argues, "impose categories on experience."

Ultimately: "Some stories are tellable but only if the teller is willing to live with existing categories for interpreting the experience." Ann Ferrell extends this notion, arguing that a tellable narrative consists of "talk (oral and written, vernacular and institutional) about the topic in the public sphere that reflects common, but often unquestioned, ideas and assumptions." Descriptions that depict Appalachians as illiterate are eminently tellable because they fit the common ideas and assumptions that have already been built up around the region. Present-day representations of Appalachia in the media as Trump Country likewise draw on these ideas and assumptions because they are at hand—they are easy to pick up and reuse. On the other hand, stories that represent Appalachians as something else—as literate, as readers and writers, as school supporters or educated people—are *untellable*. As Shuman explains: "The untellability involves a lack of recognition of the category, a 'this kind of thing doesn't happen' response." Because there is no existing set of assumptions that presents Appalachian people as readers and writers, stories that represent Appalachians in this way often spark a "'this kind of thing doesn't happen' response"—a response that often results in the experience being dismissed as the exception that proves the rule rather than as evidence that a new set of assumptions is needed in order accurately to characterize tellability so that each story that is told adds to the weight of assumptions that render other kinds of representation untellable.[4]

No one, I would argue, has added more weight to those assumptions than Jack Weller via his *Yesterday's People*. In 1965, Weller set out to identify what he considered the essential qualities of the Appalachian personality. His book, along with Harry Caudill's *Night Comes to the Cumberlands*, served to reinvigorate the idea of Appalachia in the minds of the American public in the 1960s, around the same time that Lyndon Johnson stood on a porch in Martin County, Kentucky (just down the road from the *Big Sandy News*), and declared the War on Poverty. Weller acknowledges that his experiences in Appalachia "will not fit accurately every situation, every area, or every person in the mountains," yet he proceeds to paint a portrait of the southern Appalachian as abiding by a unified set of cultural principles. Stories that contradict his essential qualities of the region aren't tellable and are thus omitted from the text, with Weller asserting that "any Appalachian person who is willing to read such a study as this hardly qualifies to be included in it." In other words, their very identity as reading Appalachians disqualifies these people from speaking meaningfully about life in their communities.[5]

To conclude his text, Weller presents a list of the characteristics of his southern Appalachian, setting it side by side with a list of middle-class American characteristics, all of which are diametrically opposed to those he identifies as Appalachian. This is perhaps the most deliberate instance of othering in writing about Appalachians as he specifically draws Appalachian life as the opposite of civilized US society. Race, culture, geographic location—all these are erased in creating a generic middle-class American who, in his imagining, fills all areas of the country outside southern Appalachia, an area that serves as a land apart from time. His list is worth reproducing here in full to demonstrate the problematic descriptions that, given their popularity and their timing, certainly influenced how the War on Poverty was waged; Ronald Eller points out that the text was "distributed to poverty workers throughout Appalachia during the War on Poverty" and "became a working manual for hundreds of antipoverty warriors and one of the most popular volumes on Appalachia in the 1960s."

Table 2. Weller's List of Southern Appalachian Characteristics

Middle-Class American	Southern Appalachian
Personal Characteristics	
1. Emphasis on community, church, clubs, etc.	1. Individualism, self-centered concerns
2. Thoughts of change and progress; expectation of change, usually for the better	2. Attitudes strongly traditionalistic
3. Freedom to determine one's life and goals	3.Fatalism
4. Routine seeker	4. Action seeker
5. Self-assurance	5. Sense of anxiety
6. No particular stress on maleness	6. Stress on traditional masculinity
7. Use of ideas, ideals, and abstractions	7. Use of anecdotes
8. Acceptance of object goals	8. Rejection of object goals
9. Oriented to progress	9. Oriented to existence
10. Strong emphasis on saving and budgeting	10. No saving or budgeting
11. Desire and ability to plan ahead carefully	11. No interest in careful long-range planning

Table 2. Weller's List of Southern Appalachian Characteristics	
Middle-Class American	Southern Appalachian
Personal Characteristics	
12. Placement of group goals above personal aims	12. Precedence of personal feelings and whims over group goals
13. Recognition of expert opinion	13. Expert opinion not recognized
Family Life Characteristics	
14. Child-centered family	14. Adult-centered family
15. Responsibility for family decisions shared by husband and wife	15. Male-dominated family
16. "Togetherness" of husband and wife	16. Separateness of husband and wife; separate reference groups
17. Home tasks shared by husband and wife	17. Sharp delineation of home tasks between husband and wife
18. Many family activities shared (vacations, amusements, etc.)	18. Few shared family activities
19. Disciplined child rearing; stress on what is thought best for the child's development	19. Permissive child rearing; stress on what pleases the child
20. Family bound by common interests as well as emotional ties	20. Family bound by emotional ties; few common interests
21. Family a bridge to outside world	21. Separation of family and outside world
Relationships with Others	
22. Reference group less important	22. Reference group most important
23. Object-oriented life patterns	23. Person-oriented life patterns
24. Association between sexes	24. Little or no association between sexes
25. Strong pressure of status	25. No status seeking
26. Striving for excellence	26. Leveling tendency in society
27. Readiness to join groups	27. Rejection of joining groups
28. Ability to function in objective ways in a group	28. Ability to function in a group only on a personal basis
29. Attachment to work; concern for job security and satisfaction	29. Detachment from work; little concern for job security or satisfaction
30. Emphasis on education	30. Ambivalence toward education
31. Cooperation with doctors, hospitals, and "outsiders"	31. Fear of doctors, hospitals, those in authority, the well educated

Table 2. Weller's List of Southern Appalachian Characteristics	
Middle-Class American	Southern Appalachian
Relationships with Others	
32. Use of government and law to achieve goals	32. Antagonism toward government and law
33. Acceptance of the world	33. Suspicion and fear of the outside world
34. Participation in organized amusements, cultural activities, etc.	34. Rejection of organized amusements, cultural activities, etc.
Source: Jack Weller, *Yesterday's People: Life in Contemporary Appalachia* (Lexington: University Press of Kentucky, 1965; reprint, Lexington: University Press of Kentucky, 2013), 161–63.	

In the introductory note to the text, Rupert Vance, a sociologist known for his studies of Appalachian society, asserts that, precisely because he is an outsider to the area who arrived as a missionary, Weller "came to know these people better than they knew themselves." This assertion, of course, contradicts Weller's own list of Appalachian traits; since Appalachians are supposedly suspicious of outsiders, those in authority, and the well educated—all attributes that describe Weller—why would his respondents have given him anything resembling the truth in their interactions? If, in other words, Weller is right about these elements of the Appalachian character, he undercuts the likely accuracy of the picture he seeks to paint.[6]

While many of Weller's claims are simply absurd (more on this below), they share one important characteristic: they serve to suggest that any problems Appalachia may have are due to its people's own personality traits. After all, how can anyone try to help if Appalachians refuse to listen to outsiders, experts, or those in authority and if they show "little concern" for job security or self-improvement? As Weller himself puts it: "The greatest challenge of Appalachia, and the most difficult, is its people." The key to the problems identified by the War on Poverty, then, must be to remedy the people themselves rather than any of the structural conditions that govern life in the region. Weller's text, above all, allows America to wash its hands of these strange and peculiar people whose problems are a result of their own anachronisms rather than structural and economic decisions made outside the region.[7]

While Weller's list and the text that supports it might themselves seem to be a quaint anachronism at this point, *Yesterday's People* was widely celebrated at the time and continues to influence perceptions of the region today.

In another media study of poverty in Beattyville, Kentucky, the *ThinkProgress* reporter Scott Rodd leans on Weller to explain why "this is what poverty looks like": "The poverty in Beattyville and many other Appalachian towns is a result of a culture holding onto its traditional values in a world that no longer shares those values. Historically, Appalachia consisted of discrete, tight-knit communities that were self-sufficient and self-sustaining. Local agriculture and tradesmen served nearby residents, and communities lost few members to the outside world. A strong, almost tribal sense of community became central to the region. In *Yesterday's People*, Jack Weller describes the ethos as a 'private system of justice based on the personal relationships common to the clan.'" Though Rodd goes on to identify the rugged terrain as an impediment to investment in the region and touches on the extract industry's decimation of the regional economy, this assertion sets the tone for the article: it is how the people respond to these challenges, not the challenges themselves, that keeps the region impoverished. No hope is held out that Beattyville will be changing any time soon, particularly because the town refuses to appreciate the value of educational opportunities properly. Rodd spends much of the article interviewing teachers and students who discuss how lack of funding and opportunity in the school system circumscribes their possibilities. Fittingly, he ends by describing Beattyville's poverty in familiar terms. He references Victor, a Beattyville native who has moved away: "[Victor] has a bleak outlook for the town's future. He paints the picture of a town that fell from prosperity into a cycle of misfortune—a cycle that, from his perspective, isn't likely to be broken."[8]

Recycling Stereotypes

The idea that Appalachians are stuck in an unbreakable cycle of poverty that is, at heart, the result of a lack of appreciation for learning (which is simply a new way to code illiteracy) is a recurring theme in both public discussion and scholarship regarding Appalachia. This theme and Weller's characteristics of southern Appalachians certainly reappear in the Trump Country coverage I discuss in the introduction. Many of the characteristics Weller lists, after all, have been reassigned to the Trump voter—although, in a sense, this is *not* a reassignment since *Trump voter* is seen as a synonym for *Appalachian* (i.e., white and rural). A multitude of opinion pieces and scholarly articles tell us that the Trump voter is a man who stresses traditional views of masculinity and see the policies of the liberal elite as an attack on traditional values (Weller's Appalachian characteristics 2 and 6). Trump voters are, at heart, anxious about their place in the world, economically and otherwise (characteristic 5). They don't appreciate expert opinions (characteristic 13) and resent the well educated (characteristic 31) as well as institutions of education (characteristic 30) because they value emotion over objective facts (characteristics 7 and 12). They distrust the government (characteristic 32) and see people from other countries as a threat to US security (characteristic 33). The most important influence of their beliefs is party affiliation, not a core set of beliefs (characteristic 22). In fact, Weller's list could easily be repackaged and marketed today as a list of characteristics of the Trump voter.[9]

The fact that Weller's list so neatly fits the many media narratives seeking to understand Trump voters suggests either that the linkage between Appalachia and Trump voters is so complete in the public mind that all Trump voters are essentially imagined as Appalachian (and vice versa) or, perhaps, that these characteristics serve less as an accurate reflection of southern Appalachian culture than a list of what qualities middle- and upper-middle-class Americans need their others to possess in order to justify their own worldviews. Since that other is now the unreadable Trump voter, this list of characteristics is simply picked up wholesale and transferred to this new group of problem causers, pulling Appalachians along for the ride.[10]

Certainly, Weller's list of characteristics of Appalachians is inconsistent with the observations elsewhere in his text, but it is also rendered inaccurate by even the slightest review of conditions in Appalachia at the time. In 1965, for instance, many Appalachians continued to rely on subsistence farming to provide at least part of the family's food supply in a given year; such farming, of course, requires the "desire and ability to plan ahead carefully," which Weller asserts Appalachians lack. While unions were rapidly losing power in Appalachia in 1965, the fact that they had served as a powerful force in the region suggests that Appalachians were willing to join groups and could "function in objective ways in a group." Moreover, their willingness to strike and even take up arms to secure better working conditions speaks to their "concern for job security and satisfaction." Some of the traits, too, that Weller notes as problematic and at odds with middle-class values make perfect sense in an Appalachian context. Weller sees the distrust of doctors as indicative of a larger distrust of authority, but doctors in coal towns were often employed by coal operators—their services were ultimately to benefit the company, not the patient, and the distrust was certainly earned in this case.[11]

Many Appalachian writers and researchers have responded to the kinds of stereotypes Weller presents by highlighting the positive qualities that are embedded within these ideas. Loyal Jones, for instance, reconceptualizes "individualism; self-centered concerns" and "separation from family and outside world" as, instead, independence and self-reliance, two admirable characteristics. Where Weller sees people for whom reference groups are less important and for whom there is a "leveling tendency" that leads away from striving for individual excellence, Jones sees an emphasis on neighborliness and humility. Weller highlights Appalachians' "antagonism toward government and law," while Jones emphasizes their patriotism and willingness to serve. In other words, for many more sympathetic commentators, the very values that Weller highlights as problems are those that are perhaps the most admirable characteristics when we imagine them in alternative terms.[12]

To put it another way, one doesn't have to know very much about Appalachia to question Weller's assertions, so the success of his book demands the question, Why were readers so willing to accept this caricature? The answer, of course, is that it fit preexisting myths about the region and its people first articulated in the 1880s. Moreover, by providing an other against which middle-class Americans could define themselves, Weller's Appalachians allowed them to celebrate their own values and simultaneously wash their hands of the problems facing Appalachia—even as their homes were built and lit cheaply because of the exploitative conditions that existed in the region. The people are the problem.

The unremitting image of Appalachian people as a problem has immense long-term effects for Appalachian residents. In particular, stereotypes about Appalachia influence how public monies are spent trying to alleviate the region's problems. If the people are the problem, then money is spent on and energy directed toward improving the people rather than the structural inequalities and the politics of development itself. Taken to extremes, this view led some to argue that the solution to Appalachia's problems was outmigration, which would provide not only a labor force for the rest of America but also jobs for those mountaineers who did not already have them. Just as important, however, it would expose Appalachians to more appropriate cultural opportunities. Eller discusses the effect of these perceptions on 1960s-era antipoverty programs developed as part of the War on Poverty. The Job Corps, he argues, "was essentially an education program whose primary goal was to teach young people how to apply for jobs" rather than a program involving skills training. Other employment programs were referred to as "our charm school" because they were based on the assumption "that people who didn't fit the established culture didn't get jobs." Likewise, Eller argues that Head Start and homemaker training programs "were designed to change the behavior of families" and that community action agencies were "tool[s] to acculturate the poor into the value system and behaviors of the middle class." Very little of the government money allocated for relieving Appalachia's poverty went to programs that sought to tackle in a more direct way the economic conditions of the region.[13]

The framing of Appalachians as problem people continues to lead to a reluctance to invest time, money, or interest in the region. In the introduction, I highlighted the Daily Kos's assertion that coal miners deserved to lose their health insurance because they voted for Trump—despite the fact that, if we actually break down voting data from coal regions, we see that many coal miners don't appear to have voted at all. This reluctance becomes evident even in the language of supportive government programs; while there is much to admire about the Obama administration's creation of "Promise Zones" for economic development, one of which encompasses southeastern Kentucky, one of the stated purposes of the Kentucky portion of the program is "decreased government spending on social programs." In other words, one reason to sponsor this program is ultimately to relieve the government of the burden of supporting Appalachians. Notably, this language is not included in descriptions of other areas designated Promise Zones, in spite of the high poverty rates of the other zones selected. It is specifically Appalachia that needs to reduce its dependency.[14]

People living in Appalachia are well aware of these attitudes, which frame their relationships with all manner of institutions, but the impacts are nowhere clearer than in their experiences within the education system. A plethora of research regarding their experiences with literacy and schooling illustrates the continued power of these stereotypes to shape how Appalachians perceive themselves and their possibilities. As one Appalachian respondent in Virginia Seitz's study of community and development puts it: "I didn't know I was poor white trash until I went to school and somebody told me. If I had never gone to school, I never would have known I was poor!" For many Appalachians, the experiences that they're told are most likely to help them escape the cycle of poverty require an acceptance and acknowledgment of their own inferiority.[15]

Todd Snyder, a professor of rhetoric and composition who identifies as Appalachian, describes similar effects of these stereotypes as he recounts an experience with his high school guidance counselor. When he attempts to ask questions about applying for college, the counselor interrupts to ask whether he has considered vocational training as a welder or asked his father to get him on at the mines. Snyder writes: "I share this memory not to suggest that my guidance counselor was a bad person or that he wasn't doing his job properly. . . . I share this memory because my counselor's advice made me feel circumscribed. He had mistaken me for a welder, a coal miner—and it hurt. His advice made me feel trapped within a particular occupational history, as if I weren't college material. To him, I was the opposite of Shakespeare's young Henry V, not a prince falling short of his great potential, but a coal miner's son overreaching his academic abilities." Snyder, of course, did make it to college and on to graduate school, but it is easy to imagine how many Appalachian students are discouraged from pursuing higher education when faced with similar questions. The futures imagined for Appalachian students—by society at large and, by extension, by the adults in their own communities—are futures that involve recycling the past: children will do what their parents and grandparents have done because that's what people do in Appalachia. Trying to break the cycle is, as we've seen, framed as a fool's errand when simply falling in step with the cycle is the easier and more familiar route.[16]

Even if Appalachians make it into higher education settings, the stereotypes that define the region predetermine their classroom performance. Sara Webb-Sunderhaus demonstrates that Appalachian students feel compelled to respond in some way to the idea of Appalachia, either by embracing its positive elements—whether or not they accurately reflect their experiences—or by positioning themselves in opposition to the hillbilly stereotype. In her study of Appalachian undergraduates, she describes a personal narrative produced in response to an assignment. Julie writes about playing in the creeks and forests near her mountain home. When Webb-Sunderhaus asks her to explain her composing process, she acknowledges that her story is partially fictional: "Yeah, I played in the woods, but I wasn't running around singing all the time or things like that. Where we lived wasn't that pretty. We lived in a run-down house. It was near the woods, but things were all torn up from the mines." She explains that she represented her experiences in this way to please her teacher: "Well, I know what people think of [her home state]. They think we all live in the mountains, that we're closer to the earth or whatever, and that we're kind of backwards. So I kind of played that up by talking about the mountains and the streams and by acting like my parents thought girls couldn't do certain things." In this case, the performance is successful—her professor loves the essay. But the success of the performance doesn't alter the fact that, in order to achieve that success, Julie is required to lean into the idea that her home is "backwards" and that her parents held her back. Other students in Webb-Sunderhaus's study work around the negative stereotypes of Appalachia by separating themselves from the stereotype while confirming them for the area as a whole. Gladys, for instance, agrees that many people in her hometown fit the "hilljack" stereotype, but she differentiates herself from them by emphasizing her cosmopolitan experiences, a process Webb-Sunderhaus likens to Goffman's stigma management. For both Gladys and Julie, the stereotypes of Appalachia influence what they feel they can say in the classroom, and, for both, being accepted in higher education is seen as requiring a degree of acceptance of those stereotypes.[17]

Evidence suggests that Julie and Gladys are right to perceive that their identity as Appalachians will affect how they are perceived in the classroom. In his study of how Appalachian dialect is perceived, Luhman found that "even university graduates with traces of Appalachian English in their speech will automatically face stereotypes of low intelligence, lack of ambition and success, and a poor education (a university degree notwithstanding)." Another study that surveyed both Appalachian and non-Appalachian teachers working in an Appalachian school district in North Carolina found that teachers hold significantly different views of students they identified as Appalachian. While the teachers typically coded these differences by describing the students as *rural* or *town*, in this particular area these distinctions broke down into Appalachian versus non-Appalachian outsiders whose families were drawn to the area by the local college and tourist industries. One teacher explained the differences in striking terms, with *Rednecks* here standing in for *Appalachian*: "The Rednecks wear the typical uniform with farm-type clothes, flannel shirts, and a cap with the name of a seed company or some chemical company on the front. They'll wear the cap religiously; you have to ask them to take it off. They chew tobacco. They use a 'Good Ol' Boy' type speech. They say 'you'uns' while the social/intellectual group never would—they'd use proper English. The intellectuals are members of the National Honors Society, the Key Club; they are the social types. They are in the 04 level classes; they'll be doctors and lawyers." Other teachers report that they are more likely to use corporal punishment on students from rural areas: "Rural students understand a whipping. You can reason with the town kids." More fundamentally, 67 percent of the high school teachers surveyed in the study acknowledged that they "treated students differently based upon their ethnic background" as Appalachian students. Appalachian students who did not fit the stereotypes of rednecks were still lumped into this group by the teachers; one student who excelled academically was still described by his teacher as a redneck from "off the back of the mountain": "He wears blue jeans, a flannel shirt, a cat-hat [Caterpillar-branded hat]. His daddy drives a pick-up truck." In other words, there was nothing Appalachians could do to escape the negative stereotypes associated with their identity as Appalachians; even success as measured by the teacher's school-based standards could not eliminate a label that subjected the student to the potential of different—worse—treatment from his teachers.[18]

James Branscombe, writing in 1978, asserts: "In an Appalachian school, the middle class aspiring teacher is just as insistent that the student be aggressive, obedient, and joyless—in short, everything the student's culture tells him he is not—as is the teacher in the Bureau of Indian Affairs school on a reservation." Kim Donehower's analysis of literacy sponsorship in an Appalachian community illustrates that this idea of "teaching out" students' Appalachian qualities, particularly their accents, remains alive and well. One of her respondents, a public school teacher, emphasizes that grammar and pronunciation "meant *so* much":

> But when they hear [incorrect grammar] at home, day in and day out, they come to school and they're wearing that there, and it's hard, you have to go over and go over, repetition, repetition, repetition, to get that—out, and then, I had a child tell me once, I had been hammering on something that I was trying to get into them, one of the students came back and said, "Ms. Sykes," said, "They made fun of me at home, because I did so and so." You know? And I said, "Well you just stick to it because *you* are *right*."

As this teacher makes clear, many Appalachian teachers see their role as preparing students to succeed by eliminating the stigmatized elements of Appalachian culture from their repertoires. These attitudes certainly remain prevalent today. To speak for a moment from my own experiences teaching a linguistics course for aspiring teachers at an institution serving primarily online Appalachian students, the students make clear that they see part of their role in Appalachian classrooms as weeding out improper language, and many express frustration with their own children who speak with Appalachian accents. This is not to insult my students, all of whom are well-meaning and are eastern Kentucky Appalachians themselves; rather, I share this example to illustrate how deeply ingrained is the idea that we must teach out students' Appalachian characteristics.[19]

Donehower's research demonstrates that the experience of the student who complained to Ms. Sykes is not unique. Schooling itself was often framed as a solution to the cultural deficiencies of the region. Donehower finds that "informants' descriptions of receiving the literacy stigmatization message at school were uniformly traumatic" and "informants' stories of having their reading and writing stigmatized because they were Appalachian were also uniformly harrowing, involving various shaming techniques on the part of the teachers." The literacy message that students received, she argues, could be paraphrased thusly: "You are starting at a disadvantage with reading and writing because you are Appalachian, and you are only going to be able to overcome it with great pain and suffering, but you had better overcome it, because otherwise you'll only be fit to live in Appalachia, a fate worse than death."[20]

Rather than subject themselves to this kind of attitude, many Appalachians are now suspicious of schooling as an institution. In her study of Appalachian college women, Katherine Kelleher Sohn documents many instances of resistance from the women's husbands and families. She attributes this reaction in part to a sense of discomfort with education more generally: "Because outsiders have caricatured Appalachian speech and culture and implied religious and cultural superiority, mountain people have adopted defensive attitudes about formal education and social mobility. . . . The promises of literacy are not the same for all, especially the working class." While this reaction is very understandable—Appalachians certainly do not need researchers to tell them that the message their children receive in schools is that their cultural heritage is almost universally negative—it serves primarily to recapitulate the very stereotypes that it responds to. It "proves," in other words, that Appalachians dislike regular schooling, are resistant to change, and distrust experts, the very qualities that the idea of Appalachia attributes to the region. Appalachian families, then, are indeed trapped in a cycle: they can keep their children in schools that denigrate their communities and heritage, or they can provide grist for the mill of the stereotypes that serve to denigrate them. No matter which option they choose, their stories will become part of the tellable narrative of Appalachia: that Appalachian people are in need of a remedy, but that, even if they manage to escape their station in life momentarily, they will inevitably cycle back to poverty, they will inevitably fall back into the narrative. Any success that they may achieve will remain untellable: it will not serve to undercut that ever-present narrative.[21]

Changing the Narrative

If individual successes are not enough to break through the narrative that characterizes Appalachia as endlessly immersed in a cycle of illiteracy and poverty, we must ask ourselves, Why does this narrative hold such power? As Ronald Eller and many others have argued, it is convenient for many people because it absolves them of responsibility for the region's problems and very deliberately creates economic conditions that work to the advantage of extract industries in the region. As William Schumann puts it: "In Appalachia, . . . powerful institutions have historically influenced the life opportunities of impoverished communities by defining them as incapable of understanding and acting on the causes of their poverty; these same cultures of institutional expertise have masked the role of outside forces in the reproduction of Appalachian inequality." In a narrative in which the people are the problem, Appalachians are to blame for their own poverty, and there is no need for a radical restructuring of an economic system that benefits those "outside forces." In a more insidious sense, illiteracy and poverty have also been monetized by those who have made a career out of solving these problems. Peter Mortensen explains: "*Il*literacy enabled the social advancement of those willing to use it as conceptual capital central to their turn-of-the-century charitable and professional enterprises. Gleaning the fields of rustic illiteracy has left a legacy no less devastating to rural livelihood than blight or drought." Eller likewise demonstrates that federal money intended to alleviate the region's problems often ends up in the hands of those local citizens and state officials who have the most invested in perpetuating the current social and economic order rather than going to programs that target the most impoverished and undereducated citizens of the region.[22]

Given the degree of investment that many groups have and have had in fostering the narrative of Appalachia as the other of America, we must tread carefully but forcefully as we articulate alternative narratives. Scholars have already offered a plethora of current and historical evidence that seeks to reimagine Appalachia in more positive terms. Yet, as current narratives around Appalachians as Trump voters suggest, there is still much work to be done in responding to the idea of Appalachia and presenting a new set of tellable narratives about the region.

I return to the voices I mention above and the omnipresence in informants' responses of the idea that an Appalachian identity is a handicap. As Donehower's commentators make clear, an Appalachian accent is perceived as a drawback; as Webb-Sunderhaus's Gladys illustrates, it is often more effective to disavow one's identity as an Appalachian or embrace its most stereotyped elements than to attempt a meaningful representation of Appalachian identity in all its complexities. The Beattyville, Kentucky, resident interviewed by Scott Rodd, Victor, speaks for many Appalachians when he describes a cycle of poverty that seems inescapable. This enduring myth colors not only outsiders' perceptions of Appalachians but also, as Erica Locklear has argued, "how Appalachian people conceive of themselves," circumscribing what residents imagine as possible and probable in their future horizons.[23]

Because so much of the current narrative around Appalachia revolves around the idea of a cycle, there are two possible ways to move beyond it. One path would be to highlight success stories—to emphasize people that have made it, who have risen from poverty or illiteracy to find success, however defined. The problems with this path are twofold. First, as we have seen, the narrative seems to have a built-in escape valve for such stories: as Weller suggests, they weren't *real* Appalachians in the first place and don't count toward the story of the region. The second potential issue is that it requires those who have success stories to stand in for an entire people, carrying a region's public representations on their backs and in their hearts. We have long recognized that this is an unfair burden to place on people who identify with minority groups, and it is unfair to place such a burden on those who identify as mountain people.

The second potential path—a recapitulation of the region's history in terms that speak directly to the falsity of the cycle narrative—have less potential for harm and may therefore be the more promising path to pursue. The cycle narrative relies on the idea that the cycle has *always existed*. This is one reason that Appalachians were so often framed as "our contemporary ancestors" at the turn of the century: describing them as such allowed any perceived deficiencies to be written backward to time immemorial rather than perceived as the result of existing social and economic pressures. The idea that Appalachians are *"yesterday's people"* further emphasizes this sense of everlastingness. One way to undercut the cycle narrative, then, is to recall and re-present a more accurate description of the past, one that undermines the notion that Appalachia has always been just as it is today or that it ever was the textless, unschooled, and illiterate place it has been represented to be.

The project of this book, then, is to attempt to provide a road map for such presentations. By recovering a history of readers and writers in the region during the period stretching from the first incursions of the extract industry to the industry's consolidation of control, I hope to provide needed evidence that the idea of Appalachia has never accurately characterized the region, particularly as the idea concerns illiteracy and a lack of education. I hope to provide an alternative tellable narrative regarding the literacy practices that were at work in these communities, and I hope that, in illustrating how community members developed imagined communities via the newspaper pages, we might find inspiration for reimagining our communities today.

The newspapers illustrate that Appalachians were even then aware of the schism between their lived realities and the myths developing about them and that they sought to respond to those perceptions in the most public forum available to them—the newspapers. We see these responses in subtle ways, as in the Torchlight's community's refutation of the idea that they keep their children at home because they oppose schooling. We also see them more directly, as when J. Wise Hagin speaks directly to fellow newspapermen who represent Breathitt County in a negative light. Throughout the papers, we can see that the idea of Appalachia has shaped Appalachians and their practices even from its earliest instantiations.

Certainly, the pages of the newspapers amply demonstrate that the idea of Appalachia did not accurately reflect the vibrant communities built around literacy practices and fostered by the newspapers. With the editors acting as sponsors of literacy and the community members working to instantiate an imagined community of readers and writers—readers and writers who are drawn from nearly every area of central Appalachia, not just Kentucky—the five papers considered in this study developed a relationship such that, as Benedict Anderson envisions, "in the minds of each [member of the community] lives the image of their communion." Working together, these readers and writers created a shared sense of purpose, interest, and goals, negotiating not only the norms that would govern the literacy practices of the newspapers but also their physical communities and interactions. In their interactions, they leave behind a record of literacy practices that clearly refute the idea of Appalachia and the myths that were articulated about their lives and experiences.[24]

The sense of communion these readers and writers shared is a powerful alternative narrative for Appalachian identity. Drawing from widely disparate areas that had shared interests and concerns, the papers brought together within one community people from many walks of life and thus with many different perspectives and put them into conversation with each other. They served to unite their interests and provide a forum for disputes to be aired and resolved. They allowed each person to imagine his or her small local area as a distinct community with its own needs and values but also to envision that community as part of a larger whole that stretched across the mountains. In this process, they illustrate not only that the mountains were literate, schooled, and filled with texts but also that they were not filled with violent people who shunned groups and valued independence above all. More than anything else, they illustrate that readers and writers envisioned themselves as part of a much larger whole, even at those moments when community norms were most up for debate.

While it is immensely difficult to unseat the current narratives surrounding Appalachia, we must begin by reimagining the histories called on to justify current perceptions and treatment of Appalachians. The vibrant community evidenced by these newspapers illustrates that the image that such histories take for granted—a cycle of illiteracy and poverty dating to the distant past—does not hold water. This helps us articulate that the current situation in much of Appalachia—in which poverty, low schooling levels, environmental degradation, and poor health do have a strong foothold—is neither a natural nor an inevitable outgrowth of a problematic past. Rather, it is the result of deliberate policies and choices—some of which can be changed, reversed, or responded to differently. If indeed current conditions are not natural or inevitable, then there are many more possibilities before us than our current narratives would suggest. Reconceiving our past and developing new tellable narratives to represent that past can allow us to "shake ourselves free, and envision alternative futures."[25]

Acknowledgments

Working in the archives can be lonely. Very often, as we read through material written decades or centuries ago, we find ourselves realizing that we may be the first to read these texts deeply since their original writers composed them. That's a nerve-wracking feeling, sometimes. What if I miss something? What if I'm not reading these texts in the way they need or were meant to be read? In reading newspapers from the late nineteenth century and the early twentieth for this project, I found myself drowning in the sheer volume of my archive, and these questions—what matters, what doesn't—were particularly pressing. I was incredibly lucky, however, because I was not alone. My mother, Denise Vibbert, read through this archive with me—just for fun, she says. Her interests differed from mine; she was less interested in literacy and schooling than race relations and the chestnut blight. Nevertheless, she kept notes for me of any references to literacy she came across, providing a double-check on my own reading of the texts, and easing my worry that I was missing something vital as I scanned through hundreds of pages of newsprint. Because she too had read these texts, she also served as a check for my conclusions: because she is as immersed in this archive as I am, I could trust that, if I were coming from left field with my ideas, she would be able to recognize my departures from the source material. This book would not exist without her, and I am very grateful.

Thanks are also due to Vanessa Kraemer Sohan, who listened to me talk about this book *every single day* during my writing of it and, despite working on her own book at the time, read each chapter and provided quick and thoughtful feedback as I wrote. Thanks to Brice Nordquist, who deserves much of the credit for the completion of this project. I started this research eight years ago, and I set it aside as life happened, including the birth of my triplets. As I moved from full-time to adjunct work, Brice is the person who kept me involved in the field and pushed me back into full-time work, providing me with the impetus finally to pick this research up again and see it through to completion. Without that necessary push, this book would never have been finished. Like Vanessa, he also listened to me chat about this book much more than can possibly have been interesting. Lisa

Arnold and Carol Mattingly also deserve thanks for reading drafts of this work, starting eight years ago and continuing through to its current form. Anne Dean Dotson has been an enthusiastic and helpful editor throughout the process, and I appreciate her care with my work. I also want to thank my in-laws, John and Judy NeCamp, and my father, John Vibbert, for helping provide the time I needed to work on this project. Finally, thanks are due to my husband, John NeCamp, who has provided every possible kind of support—emotional, financial, and otherwise—as I did this work as a student, a professor, a full-time mom, and back again. I could not ask for a more thoughtful partner.

Notes

Introduction

1. Claire Galofaro, "In the Heart of Trump Country, His Base's Faith Is Unshaken," AP News, December 27, 2017, https://apnews.com/ee19ceb7cf0d4af4ab73c393708148bf.

2. Roger Cohen, "We Need 'Somebody Spectacular': Views from Trump Country," *New York Times*, September 9, 2016, https://www.nytimes.com/2016/09/11/opinion/sunday/we-need-somebody-spectacular-views-from-trump-country.html; Jeff Saward, "Welcome to Trump Country, U.S.A.," *Vanity Fair*, February 24, 2016, https://www.vanityfair.com/news/2016/02/donald-trump-supporters-west-virginia.

3. Ronald D. Eller, foreword to *Back Talk from Appalachia: Confronting Stereotypes*, ed. Dwight B. Billings, Gurney Norman, and Katherine Ledford (Lexington: University Press of Kentucky, 1999), ix–xi, ix; Chris McGreal, "America's Poorest White Town: Abandoned by Coal, Swallowed by Drugs," *The Guardian*, November 12, 2015, https://www.theguardian.com/us-news/2015/nov/12/beattyville-kentucky-and-americas-poorest-towns. See also Samantha NeCamp, "The *Hazel Green Herald* and the 'Idea of Appalachia,'" *Journal of Appalachian Studies* 17, no. 2 (2011): 66–84, 66.

4. Henry Shapiro, *Appalachia on Our Mind: The Southern Mountains and the Mountaineer in the American Consciousness, 1870–1920* (Chapel Hill: University of North Carolina Press, 1978), 3 (quoting Harney); "Be Happy for Coal Miners Losing Their Health Insurance. They're Getting Exactly What They Voted For," Daily Kos, December 12, 2016, https://www.dailykos.com/stories/2016/12/12/1610198/-Be-happy-for-coal-miners-losing-their-health-insurance-They-re-getting-exactly-what-they-voted-for; Frank Rich, "No Sympathy for the Hillbilly," *New York Magazine*, March 9, 2017, http://nymag.com/daily/intelligencer/2017/03/frank-rich-no-sympathy-for-the-hillbilly.html.

5. Elizabeth Hagedorn, "This Is What Victory Looks Like in the Most Pro-Trump County in America," *Circa*, November 9, 2016, https://www.circa.com/story/2016/11/09/politics/this-is-what-victory-looks-like-in-the-most-pro-trump-county-in-america (link no longer active). For information on the lack of working-class Trump voters, see Nicholas Carnes and Noam Lupu, "It's Time to Bust the Myth: Most Trump Voters Were Not Working Class," *Washington Post*, June 5, 2017, https://www.washingtonpost.com/news/monkey-cage/wp/2017/06/05/its-time-to-bust-the-myth-most-trump-voters-were-not-working-class/?utm_term=.7322a1181e94. For voting statistics for West Virginia, see "2016 West Virginia Presidential Election Results," *Politico*, December 13, 2016, https://www.politico.com/2016-election/results/map/president/west-virginia; and "2016 General Election Turnout," West Virginia Secretary of State Office, 2018, https://sos.wv.gov/elections/Documents/HistVoteTurnoutDocs/2016General.pdf. Nationally,

voter turnout was approximately 55 percent of eligible voters. See Gregory Wallace, "Voter Turnout at 20-Year Low in 2016," CNN, November 30, 2016, https://www.cnn.com/2016/11/11/politics/popular-vote-turnout-2016/index.html.

6. Kim Donehower, "How to Reread Appalachian Literacy Research," in *Rereading Appalachia: Literacy, Place, and Cultural Resistance,* ed. Sara Webb-Sunderhaus and Kim Donehower (Lexington: University Press of Kentucky, 2015), 13–32, 14; Kevin Baker, "The Eternal Sunshine of the Spotless White Mind," *New Republic,* March 18, 2017, https://newrepublic.com/article/141435/eternal-sunshine-spotless-white-mind.

7. Ronald Lewis, "Beyond Isolation and Homogeneity: Diversity and the History of Appalachia," in Billings, Norman, and Ledford, eds., *Back Talk from Appalachia,* 21–44, 22; Mary Beth Pudup, Dwight Billings, and Altina Waller, *Appalachia in the Making: The Mountain South in the Nineteenth Century* (Chapel Hill: University of North Carolina Press, 1995), 4; Shapiro, *Appalachia on Our Mind,* x–xi; Samantha NeCamp, *Adult Literacy and American Identity: The Moonlight Schools and Americanization Programs* (Carbondale: Southern Illinois University Press, 2014); John Williams, *Appalachia: A History* (Chapel Hill: University North Carolina Press, 2002), 9.

8. Lee Soltow and Edward Stevens, *The Rise of Literacy and the Common School in the United States: A Socioeconomic Analysis to 1870* (Chicago: University of Chicago Press, 1981), 23, 185; Arnold Toynbee, *A Study of History: Abridgment of Volumes I–VI by D. C. Somervell* (Oxford: Oxford University Press, 1947), 149; David Looff, *Appalachia's Children: The Challenge of Mental Health* (Lexington: University Press of Kentucky, 1971), 16, 159; Cora Wilson Stewart, *Moonlight Schools: For the Emancipation of Adult Illiterates* (New York: Dutton, 1922), 12; John Fox Jr., *The Kentuckians: A Knight of the Cumberland* (New York: Scribner, 1909), 56. See also NeCamp, "The *Hazel Green Herald* and the 'Idea of Appalachia,'" 67–68.

9. See NeCamp, "The *Hazel Green Herald* and the 'Idea of Appalachia.'" For information on Appalachia's backwardness and isolation or lack thereof, see Ronald Lewis, *Transforming the Appalachian Countryside: Railroads, Deforestation, and Social Change in West Virginia, 1880–1920* (Chapel Hill: University of North Carolina Press, 1998); Pudup, Billings, and Waller, *Appalachia in the Making;* Altina Waller, *Feud: Hatfields, McCoys, and Social Change in Appalachia, 1860–1900* (Chapel Hill: University of North Carolina Press, 1988); and Williams, *Appalachia.* For information on the origins of the idea of Appalachia, see Mark Banker, *Appalachians All: East Tennesseans and the Elusive History of an American Region* (Knoxville: University of Tennessee Press, 2010); Allen Batteau, *The Invention of Appalachia* (Tucson: University of Arizona Press, 1990); Richard Drake, *A History of Appalachia* (Lexington: University Press of Kentucky, 2001); Elizabeth Engelhardt, "Writing That Old Moonshine Lit: Gender, Power, and Nation in Unexpected Places," *Journal of Appalachian Studies* 13, nos. 1–2 (2007): 49–74; Stewart Plein, "Portraits of Appalachia: The Identification of Stereotype in Publisher's Bookbindings, 1850–1915," *Journal of Appalachian Studies* 15, nos. 1–2 (2009): 99–115; Pudup, Billings, and Waller, *Appalachia in the Making;* Shapiro, *Appalachia on Our Mind;* and Williams, *Appalachia.*

10. "County Courthouse Disasters in Kentucky," Kentucky Department of Librar-

ies and Archives, 2018, https://kdla.ky.gov/researchers/Pages/courthousedisasters.aspx.

11. Donehower, "How to Reread Appalachian Literacy Research," 3; Sara Webb-Sunderhaus, "Rhetorical Theories of Appalachian Literacies," in Webb-Sunderhaus and Donehower, eds., *Rereading Appalachian Stereotypes,* 179–98, 187. For further discussion of the lack of archival materials available in Appalachia, see Emma Howse, "Appalachian Identities and the Difficulties of Archival Literacy Research," in Webb-Sunderhaus and Donehower, eds., *Rereading Appalachian Stereotypes,* 55–76.

12. Jennifer Sinor, *The Extraordinary Work of Ordinary Writing: Annie Ray's Diary* (Iowa City: University of Iowa Press, 2002), 3.

13. Charles B. Keeney, "The Battle of Blair Mountain Is Still Being Waged," Cultural Landscape Foundation, February 26, 2018, https://tclf.org/battle-blair-mountain-still-being-waged; Ron Soodalter, "In the Battle of Blair Mountain, Coal Is Threatening to Bury Labor History," *The Progressive,* January 31, 2018, http://progressive.org/magazine/the-battle-over-blair-mountain-famous-labor-site.

14. Eller, foreword, x; Baker, "The Eternal Sunshine of the Spotless White Mind."

15. McGreal, "America's Poorest White Town"; Soltow and Stevens, *The Rise of Literacy and the Common School in the United States,* 185.

16. Yuval Noah Harari, *Sapiens: A Brief History of Humankind* (New York: Harper's, 2015), 241.

17. Alexis de Tocqueville, *Democracy in America,* trans. Arthur Goldhammer (New York: Penguin Putnam, 2004), 600; Benedict Anderson, *Imagined Communities: Reflections on the Origin and Spread of Nationalism* (London: Verso, 1983; reprint, London; Verso, 2016), 6, 35.

18. Anderson, *Imagined Communities;* Tocqueville, *Democracy in America;* Jessica Enoch, *Refiguring Rhetorical Education: Women Teaching African American, Native American, and Chicano/a Students, 1865–1911* (Carbondale: Southern Illinois University Press, 2008); James Parins, *Literacy and Intellectual Life in the Cherokee Nation, 1820–1906* (Norman: University of Oklahoma Press, 2013); Alicia Brazeau, *Circulating Literacy: Writing Instruction in American Periodicals, 1880–1910* (Carbondale: Southern Illinois University Press, 2016), 3.

19. Deborah Brandt, "Sponsors of Literacy," *College Composition and Communication* 49, no. 2 (1998): 165–85, 166, 167.

20. Brandt, "Sponsors of Literacy," 167; George Payne, *History of Journalism in the United States* (New York: D. Appleton, 1924).

1. Recovering Literacy

1. Batteau, *The Invention of Appalachia;* Shapiro, *Appalachia on Our Mind;* Drake, *A History of Appalachia.* The *Concise Oxford Companion to American Literature* defines *local color writing* as writing in which "one finds the dual influence of romanticism and realism, since the author frequently looks away from ordinary life to distant lands, strange customs, or exotic scenes, but retains through minute detail a sense of fidelity and accuracy of description." *Concise Oxford Companion to*

American Literature, ed. James Hart (Oxford: Oxford University Press, 2002), 230. It is worth noting that, while coal is most often associated with Appalachia, timber and oil interests were also present.

2. Mary Noailles Murfree, *In the Tennessee Mountains* (London: Longmans, Green, 1884).

3. "The Appalachian Region," Appalachian Regional Commission, n.d., https://www.arc.gov/appalachian_region/TheAppalachianRegion.asp.

4. John Williams, "Counting Yesterday's People: Using Aggregate Data to Address the Problem of Appalachia's Boundaries," *Journal of Appalachian Studies* 2, no. 1 (1996): 3–27, 4, and *Appalachia,* 12.

5. James Lane Allen, *The Blue-Grass Region of Kentucky and Other Kentucky Articles* (New York: Harper & Bros., 1892); Williams, *Appalachia.*

6. Anderson, *Imagined Communities.*

7. See also NeCamp, "The *Hazel Green Herald* and the 'Idea of Appalachia,'" 70.

8. Harvey Graff, *The Legacies of Literacy: Continuities and Contradictions in Western Culture and Society* (Bloomington: Indiana University Press, 1991), 3; Paul Prior and Jody Shipka, "Chronotopic Lamination: Tracing the Contours of Literate Activity," in *Writing Selves/Writing Societies,* ed. Charles Bazerman and David Russell (Fort Collins, CO: WAC Clearinghouse, 2003), 180–238, 181, https://wac.colostate.edu/books/perspectives/selves-societies; Deborah Brandt, *Literacy in American Lives* (Cambridge: Cambridge University Press, 2001), 4–5.

9. "About the *Big Sandy News.* (Louisa, Ky.) 1885–1929," Chronicling America: Historic American Newspapers, Library of Congress, 2018, https://chroniclingamerica.loc.gov/lccn/sn83004226.

10. US Census Bureau, *1880 Census* (Washington, DC: National Archives and Records Administration, 1880), https://search.ancestry.com/search/db.aspx?dbid=6742.

11. The Hazel Green Academy remained open until 1983. Calvin P. Jones, "National Register of Historic Places Inventory—Nomination Form," US Department of the Interior, 1978, https://npgallery.nps.gov/NRHP/GetAsset/NRHP/79001047_text; US Census Bureau, *1880 Census.*

12. "About the *Hazel Green Herald.* (Hazel Green, Wolfe County, Ky.) 1885–19??," Chronicling America: Historic American Newspapers, Library of Congress, 2018, https://chroniclingamerica.loc.gov/lccn/sn86063242; *Hazel Green Herald,* March 4, 1885. See also NeCamp, "The *Hazel Green Herald* and the 'Idea of Appalachia.'"

13. Union College continues to operate as a private Methodist college in Barbourville today.

14. "About *Mountain Advocate.* (Barbourville, Ky.) 1904–1935," Chronicling America: Historic American Newspapers, Library of Congress, 2018, https://chroniclingamerica.loc.gov/lccn/sn87060032. Unfortunately, none of the competing papers seem to have been preserved. US Census Bureau, *1900 Census* (Washington, DC: National Archives and Records Administration, 1900), https://search.ancestry.com/search/db.aspx?dbid=7602.

15. "About the *Clay City Times.* (Clay City, Ky.) 1901–Current," Chronicling America: Historic American Newspapers, Library of Congress, 2018, https://chroniclingamerica.loc.gov/lccn/sn86069657.

16. T. R. C. Hutton, *Bloody Breathitt: Politics and Violence in the Appalachian South* (Lexington: University Press of Kentucky, 2015), 1, 4.

17. Hutton, *Bloody Breathitt.*

18. Brandt, "Sponsors of Literacy," 166.

2. Sponsoring Literacy in Appalachia

1. The northern women who taught in coal and timber camps have left behind relatively little archival evidence of their practices and beliefs, and there is little scholarly literature surrounding them. They are represented sympathetically but with a slightly jaundiced eye in many fictional texts, including Lee Smith's *Fair and Tender Ladies* (New York: Pan, 1988) and Diane Gilliam Fisher's *Kettle Bottom* (Florence, MA: Perugia, 2004).

2. Donehower, "How to Reread Appalachian Literacy Research," 2.

3. Michael Schudson, "Toward a Troubleshooting Manual for Journalism History," *Journalism and Mass Communication Quarterly* 74, no. 3 (1997): 463–76, 472. See also NeCamp, "The *Hazel Green Herald* and the 'Idea of Appalachia,'" 70.

4. Schudson, "Toward a Troubleshooting Manual for Journalism History," 472. See also NeCamp, "The *Hazel Green Herald* and the 'Idea of Appalachia,'" 71; Payne, *History of Journalism in the United States,* 242; and "About the *Clay City Times.*" The exception to these statements is the *Big Sandy News,* which existed in a different town and under a different name prior to its purchase. The eventual owner, Milton Conley, refocused and renamed the paper to create the *News,* seemingly in response to local interest.

5. Anderson, *Imagined Communities,* 6; Sandra Gabriele and Paul Moore, "The *Globe* on Saturday, the *World* on Sunday: Toronto Weekend Editions and the Influence of the American Sunday Paper, 1886–1895," *Canadian Journal of Communication* 34, no. 3 (2009): 337–58, 352. Portions of this paragraph first appeared in NeCamp, "The *Hazel Green Herald* and the 'Idea of Appalachia,'" 69.

6. *Hazel Green Herald,* March 4, 1885.

7. *Mountain Advocate,* February 19, 1904.

8. *Clay City Times,* December 12, 1901.

9. *Big Sandy News,* February 10, 1911, September 22, 1887.

10. *Big Sandy News,* June 17, 1886, June 23, 1887; *Hazel Green Herald,* January 2, 1908.

11. *Clay City Times,* December 26, 1901.

12. *Hazel Green Herald,* March 30, 1887; *Clay City Times,* December 12, 1901; *Breathitt County News,* February 2, 1906; *Mountain Advocate,* February 26, 1904; *Clay City Times,* December 12, 1901.

13. *Clay City Times,* November 28, 1901.

14. *Big Sandy News,* September 30, 1910.

15. *Hazel Green Herald,* March 4, 1885. Parts of this paragraph first appeared in NeCamp, "The *Hazel Green Herald* and the 'Idea of Appalachia,'" 72.

16. *Mountain Advocate,* May 12, 1905; *Big Sandy News,* May 13, 1886; *Hazel Green Herald,* September 24, 1908; *Big Sandy News,* August 2, 1907.

17. *Clay City Times,* November 28, 1901.

18. *Mountain Advocate,* July 11, 1919.

19. Carl Osthaus, *Partisans of the Southern Press: Editorial Spokesmen of the Nineteenth Century* (Lexington: University Press of Kentucky, 1994), 166; *Hazel Green Herald,* August 24, 1885, March 11, 1885. See also NeCamp, "The *Hazel Green Herald* and the 'Idea of Appalachia,'" 73.

20. *Breathitt County News,* January 6, 1905.

21. See NeCamp, "The *Hazel Green Herald* and the 'Idea of Appalachia,'" 76.

22. It is likely that all the papers used the same advertising service given the similarities in the advertisements they carried, but only these three make explicit reference to how ads were obtained. For an example of the Standard Oil advertisement, see *Big Sandy News,* March 22, 1912.

23. *Hazel Green Herald,* December 2, 1886, 3, December 23, 1887.

24. *Hazel Green Herald,* June 4, 1885. The *Herald* featured syndicated reviews of a variety of texts. In the issue in which this article appears, e.g., there are also brief discussions of "the ephemeral poets of a generation or two ago," including Grenville Mellen, and a newly published "Dictionary of Authors." The other papers do include similar pieces, but the *Herald* features them much more regularly. I speculate that this is due to the emphasis on literature at the Hazel Green Academy. This paragraph first appeared in NeCamp, "The *Hazel Green Herald* and the 'Idea of Appalachia,'" 80–81.

25. Patricia Okker, *Social Stories: The Magazine Novel in Nineteenth-Century America* (Charlottesville: University of Virginia Press, 2003), 3, 15.

26. *Mountain Advocate,* February 21, 1913.

27. *Clay City Times,* May 4, 1905.

28. *Big Sandy News,* September 16, 1886; *Hazel Green Herald,* November 12, 1908; *Big Sandy News,* November 23, 1906, August 24, 1906. *O-be-joyful* was a slang term for alcohol commonly used during the Civil War. For information on the *Courier-Journal*'s endorsements, see Osthaus, *Partisans of the Southern Press;* and Herndon J. Evans, *The Newspaper Press of Kentucky* (Lexington: University Press of Kentucky, 1976; reprint, Lexington: University Press of Kentucky, 2009).

29. *Clay City Times,* December 19, 1901; *Hazel Green Herald,* September, 5 1907.

30. *Big Sandy News,* August 26, 1886.

31. *Breathitt County News,* February 17, 1905. For further discussion of the literacy myth, see Harvey Graff, *The Literacy Myth: Cultural Integration and Social Structure in the Nineteenth Century* (New York: Academic, 1979; reprint, New York: Routledge, 2017).

3. Writing a Community

1. Deborah Brandt, *The Rise of Writing: Redefining Mass Literacy* (Cambridge: Cambridge University Press, 2014), 1, 2; Tocqueville, *Democracy in America,* 600.

2. Brandt, *The Rise of Writing,* 2. For a further exploration of the connection between literacy and perceived morality, see Graff, *The Literacy Myth.*

3. *Clay City Times,* January 5, 1905.

4. *Hazel Green Herald,* March 18, 1885; *Mountain Advocate,* September 5, 1913; *Hazel Green Herald,* March 18, 1885; *Clay City Times,* June 5, 1919.

5. *Mountain Advocate,* March 21, 1919; *Hazel Green Herald,* March 6, 1902; *Mountain Advocate,* March 21, 1919; *Clay City Times,* December 18, 1913.

6. Sarah Pedersen, "What's in a Name? The Revealing Use of Nom de Plumes in Women's Correspondence to Daily Newspapers in Edwardian Scotland," *Media History* 10, no. 3 (2004): 175–85.

7. Differences in political leanings were especially marked in Breathitt County, where such differences led, as we have seen, to murder.

8. *Mountain Advocate,* June 3, 1904.

9. *Big Sandy News,* January 19, 1912.

10. *Big Sandy News,* December 23, 1904; *Clay City Times,* June 5, 1919.

11. *Clay City Times,* July 10, 1913; *Big Sandy News,* May 12, 1890.

12. *Big Sandy News,* February 3, 1905; *Big Sandy News,* January 27, 1905.

13. *Big Sandy News,* February 3, 1905.

14. *Mountain Advocate,* July 22, 1904, July 15, 1904.

15. *Clay City Times,* April 17, 1913.

16. *Hazel Green Herald,* May 13, 1885. Portions of this paragraph appear in NeCamp, "The *Hazel Green Herald* and the 'Idea of Appalachia,'" 78–79.

17. *Hazel Green Herald,* May 27, 1885, March 30, 1887. Portions of this paragraph appear in NeCamp, "The *Hazel Green Herald* and the 'Idea of Appalachia,'" 79.

18. *Mountain Advocate,* January 28, 1910.

19. *Breathitt County News,* June 28, 1907.

20. Much like the Bloody Breathitt feuds, the French-Eversole feud is commonly attributed to hot tempers and inappropriate relationships—in this case, a romantic affair—but in reality was the result of disagreements over coal rights and business practices. See John Ed Pearce, *Days of Darkness: The Feuds of Eastern Kentucky* (Lexington: University Press of Kentucky, 1994).

21. *Big Sandy News,* April 21, 1911.

22. *Clay City Times,* July 13, 1916.

23. *Clay City Times,* August 31, 1905.

24. *Breathitt County News,* February 17, 1905.

25. *Clay City Times,* April 9, 1903.

26. *Mountain Advocate,* July 15, 1904.

27. For further discussion of the myth of Appalachia as tradition bound and unchanging, see Williams, *Appalachia.*

4. Schooling Appalachia

1. Catherine Marshall, *Christy* (New York: McGraw-Hill, 1967). For information on the Hindman Settlement School, see Sarah Jordan Bowles, "Troublesome Inven-

tions: The Rhetoric of the Hindman Settlement School, 1902–1927" (PhD diss., Miami University, 2008); Patricia Kahn, "How the Social Reform Movement Impacted Handiwork at Hindman Settlement School in Hindman, Kentucky during 1902–1920" (PhD diss., Ohio State University, 2003); Jess Stoddart, *Challenge and Change in Appalachia: The Story of the Hindman Settlement School* (Lexington: University Press of Kentucky, 2002), and *The Quare Women's Journals: May Stone and Katherine Pettit's Summers in the Kentucky Mountains and the Founding of the Hindman Settlement School* (Frankfort, KY: Jesse Stuart Foundation, 1997); and David Whisnant, *All That Is Native and Fine: The Politics of Culture in an American Region* (Chapel Hill: University of North Carolina Press, 1984). For studies of the Moonlight Schools, see Yvonne Honeycutt Baldwin, *Cora Wilson Stewart and Kentucky's Moonlight Schools: Fighting for Literacy in America* (Lexington: University Press of Kentucky, 2006); Krista Bryson, "Conflicted Rhetorics of Appalachian Identity in the Kentucky Moonlight Schools," in Webb-Sunderhaus and Donehower, eds., *Rereading Appalachian Stereotypes*, 179–98; Jane Greer, "Expanding Working-Class Rhetorical Traditions: The Moonlight Schools and Alternative Solidarities among Appalachian Women, 1911–1920," *College English* 77, no. 3 (2015): 216–35; NeCamp, *Adult Literacy and American Identity;* and Willie Nelms, *Cora Wilson Stewart: Crusader against Illiteracy* (Jefferson, NC: McFarland, 1997). For information on the Highlander Folk School, see Dennis Keefe, "Andragogy in the Appalachians: Myles Horton, the Highlander Folk School, and Education for Social and Economic Justice," *International Journal of Adult Vocational Education and Technology* 6, no. 3 (2015): 16–30; Stephen Schneider, *You Can't Padlock an Idea: Rhetorical Education at the Highlander Folk School, 1932–1961* (Columbia: University of South Carolina Press, 2014); Wendy Soltz, "Just Miles Away but Worlds Apart: Examining Jewish Participation in Integration Programs at Black Mountain College and Highlander Folk School, 1933–1964," *Association for Jewish Studies Review* 41, no. 1 (2017): 203–33; and Barbara J. Thayer-Bacon, "An Exploration of Myles Horton's Democratic Praxis: Highlander Folk School," *Journal of Educational Foundations* 18, no. 2 (2004): 5–23.

2. Looff, *Appalachia's Children*, 16, 159; Victoria Purcell-Gates, *Other People's Words: The Cycle of Low Literacy* (Cambridge, MA: Harvard University Press, 1995); J. D. Vance, *Hillbilly Elegy: A Memoir of a Family and Culture in Crisis* (New York: Harper, 2016).

3. For more information on the appeals used to fund settlement schools, see Stoddart, *Challenge and Change in Appalachia.*

4. *Big Sandy News,* June 23, 1887, March 29,1888; William Ellis, *A History of Education in Kentucky* (Lexington: University Press of Kentucky, 2011), 77.

5. *Big Sandy News,* September 24, 1885; *Clay City Times,* July 3, 1902, July 17, 1902.

6. *Big Sandy News,* January 19, 1906; *Clay City Times,* January 11, 1917; *Mountain Advocate,* July 22, 1904.

7. *Clay City Times,* August 31, 1916, January 31, 1918, January 26, 1911.

8. *Big Sandy News,* August 14, 1908.

9. *Clay City Times,* July 19, 1917; Ellis, *A History of Education in Kentucky,* 106.

10. *Clay City Times,* January 14, 1915; Ellis, *A History of Education in Kentucky.*

11. *Breathitt County News,* February 12, 1909; *Big Sandy News,* February 3, 1905.

12. *Clay City Times,* February 11, 1904, September 16, 1915, February 9, 1905.

13. *Hazel Green Herald,* December 26, 1907; *Clay City Times,* December 29, 1904.

14. *Clay City Times,* August 31, 1905; *Big Sandy News,* February 23, 1906. Teachers were elected in the sense that the board of trustees for the school district voted on candidates.

15. *Big Sandy News,* September 13, 1912; *Mountain Advocate,* April 25, 1919.

16. *Big Sandy News,* April 29, 1910, May 25, 1906, February 23, 1906.

17. *Clay City Times,* January 23, 1902.

18. *Big Sandy News,* September 30, 1910.

19. *Big Sandy News,* September 4, 1908, June 8, 1906, July 22, 1886.

20. *Big Sandy News,* July 14, 1911.

21. *Big Sandy News,* September 13, 1912; *Clay City Times,* December 18, 1913.

22. *Clay City Times,* July 10, 1913.

23. *Hazel Green Herald,* March 19, 1908; *Breathitt County News,* November 17, 1905; *Clay City Times,* September 2, 1909.

24. Graff, *The Literacy Myth,* 15.

25. *Big Sandy News,* November 4, 1910.

26. For more information on how Moonlight School students were represented in the news, see NeCamp, *Adult Literacy and American Identity.*

27. *Big Sandy News,* January 19, 1912.

28. Stoddart, *Challenge and Change in Appalachia,* 17.

29. Erica Abrams Locklear, *Negotiating a Perilous Empowerment: Appalachian Women's Literacies* (Athens: Ohio University Press, 2011), 24; Yuval Noah Harari, *Homo Deus* (New York: Harper's, 2017), 59–60.

Conclusion

1. Harari, *Sapiens,* 241; Harari, *Homo Deus,* 60.

2. Purcell-Gates, *Other People's Words;* Soltow and Stevens, *The Rise of Literacy and the Common School in the United States,* 185; Robert Schenkkan, *The Kentucky Cycle* (New York: Plume, 1992); Marisol Bello, "No Victory in War on Poverty in Eastern Kentucky," *USA Today,* January 25, 2014, https://www.usatoday.com/story/news/nation/2014/01/25/war-on-poverty-50th-anniversary/4326109.

3. Jack Weller, *Yesterday's People: Life in Contemporary Appalachia* (Lexington: University Press of Kentucky, 1965; reprint, Lexington: University Press of Kentucky, 2013), 161. See also Williams, *Appalachia.*

4. Sara Webb-Sunderhaus, "'Keep the Appalachian, Drop the Redneck': Tellable Student Narratives of Appalachian Identity," *College English* 73, no. 1 (2016): 11–33; Amy Shuman, *Other People's Stories: Entitlement Claims and the Critique of Empathy* (Urbana: University of Illinois Press, 2010), 8–9; Ann Ferrell, "'It's Really Hard to Tell the

True Story of Tobacco': Stigma, Tellability, and Reflexive Scholarship," *Journal of Folklore Research* 49, no. 2 (2012): 127–52, 128; Shuman, *Other People's Stories,* 19.

5. Harry Caudill, *Night Comes to the Cumberlands: A Biography of a Depressed Area* (New York: Little, Brown, 1963); Weller, *Yesterday's People,* 5.

6. Ronald D. Eller, *Uneven Ground: Appalachia since 1945* (Lexington: University Press of Kentucky, 2008), 102; Weller, *Yesterday's People,* 161–63; Rupert Vance, "An Introductory Note," in *Yesterday's People: Life in Contemporary Appalachia,* by Jack Weller (Lexington: University Press of Kentucky, 1965; reprint, Lexington: University Press of Kentucky, 2013), ix–xii, ix.

7. Weller, *Yesterday's People,* 7.

8. Scott Rodd, "This Is What Poverty Looks Like," *ThinkProgress,* March 11, 2015, https://thinkprogress.org/this-is-what-poverty-looks-like-5218e194d4fe.

9. Weller, *Yesterday's People,* 161–63. For opinion and scholarly writing about Trump voters' disdain for the liberal elite and their traditional views of masculinity, see Emily K. Carian and Tagart Cain Sobotka, "Playing the Trump Card: Masculinity Threat and the U. S. 2016 Presidential Election," *Socius,* January 2018, doi:10.1177/2378023117740699; J. Oliver Conroy, "'Angry White Men': The Sociologist Who Studied Trump's Base Before Trump," *The Guardian,* February 27, 2017, https://www.theguardian.com/world/2017/feb/27/michael-kimmel-masculinity-far-right-angry-white-men; McKay Coppins, "'You Need to Think about It Like a War,'" *The Atlantic,* December 7, 2017, https://www.theatlantic.com/politics/archive/2017/12/the-vanishing-values-voter/547772; Emily Ekins, "The Five Types of Trump Voters: Who They Are and What They Believe," Democracy Fund Voter Study Group, June 2017, https://www.voterstudygroup.org/publications/2016-elections/the-five-types-trump-voters; Jill Filipovic, "What Donald Trump Thinks It Takes to Be a Man," *New York Times,* November 2, 2018, https://www.nytimes.com/2017/11/02/opinion/sunday/donald-trump-masculinity.html; Tom Jacobs, "Inside the Mind of Hardcore Trump Supporters," *Pacific Standard,* February 15, 2018, https://psmag.com/news/inside-the-minds-of-hardcore-trump-supporters; Paul Elliott Johnson, "The Art of Masculine Victimhood: Donald Trump's Demagoguery," *Women's Studies in Communication* 40, no. 3 (2017): 229–50; Olga Kazan, "The Precarious Masculinity of 2016 Voters," *The Atlantic,* October 12, 2016, https://www.theatlantic.com/politics/archive/2016/10/male-trump-voters-masculinity/503741; and Ryne Sherman, "Personal Values and Support for Donald Trump during the 2016 US Presidential Primary," *Personality and Individual Differences* 128, no. 1 (2018): 33–38. For articles discussing Trump voters' anxiety, economic and otherwise, see Daniel Cox, Rachel Lienesch, and Robert Jones, "Beyond Economics: Fears of Cultural Displacement Pushed the White Working Class to Trump," PRRI, May 9, 2017, https://www.prri.org/research/white-working-class-attitudes-economy-trade-immigration-election-donald-trump; Jed Kolko, "Trump Was Stronger Where the Economy Is Weaker," *FiveThirtyEight,* November 10, 2016, https://fivethirtyeight.com/features/trump-was-stronger-where-the-economy-is-weaker; Diana Mutz, "Status Threat, Not Economic Hardship, Explains 2016 Presidential Vote," *Proceedings of the National Academy of*

Sciences of the United States of America, vol. 115, no. 19 (2018), http://www.pnas.org/content/115/19/E4330; and David West, "The Economic Anxiety That Helped Fuel Trump's Rise Isn't Going Away, and Neither Is Trumpism," NBC News, April 21, 2018, https://www.nbcnews.com/think/opinion/economic-anxiety-helped-fuel-trump-s-rise-isn-t-going-ncna866816. For articles that focus on Trump voters' attitudes toward expert opinions, institutions of education, and emotion over facts, see Ariel Edwards-Levy, "Americans Don't Think the Government Needs 'Experts,'" *Huffington Post,* December 8, 2016, https://www.huffingtonpost.com/entry/poll-civil-service-experts_us_5849d515e4b04c8e2baeede9; Phillip Erickson, "Baylor Researchers Examine Trump Voters, Religious Values," *Waco Tribune-Herald,* September 7, 2017, http://www.wacotrib.com/news/higher education/baylor-researchers-examine-trump-voters-religious-values/article_24adfb74-64a3-5543-a11a-5580856b7229.html; Richard Fording and Sanford Schram, "The Cognitive and Emotional Sources of Trump Support: The Case of Low-Information Voters," *New Political Science* 39, no. 4 (2017): 670–86; Matt Motta, "Had Enough of Experts? Anti-Intellectualism Is Linked to Voters' Support for Movements That Are Skeptical of Expertise," LSE USCentre, August 30, 2017, http://blogs.lse.ac.uk/usappblog/2017/08/30/had-enough-of-experts-anti-intellectualism-is-linked-to-voters-support-for-movements-that-are-skeptical-of-expertise; Tom Nichols, "Trump Is Delivering What He Promised: A Government with No Experts," *Washington Post,* March 8, 2018, https://www.washingtonpost.com/news/posteverything/wp/2018/03/08/president-trump-is-delivering-what-he-promised-a-government-with-no-experts/?utm_term=.4a0a61c4449e; Chris Riotta, "Majority of Republicans Say Colleges Are Bad for America (Yes, Really!)," *Newsweek,* July 10, 2017, http://www.newsweek.com/republicans-believe-college-education-bad-america-donald-trump-media-fake-news-634474; and Javier Rivas, "Our Experiment into How Voters Think Shows That They Go with Their Guts," *The Conversation,* January 18, 2018, http://theconversation.com/our-experiment-into-how-voters-think-shows-that-they-go-with-their-guts-90241. For articles about Trump voters' xenophobia and distrust of government, see Uri Friedman, "Why Trump Is Thriving in an Age of Distrust," *The Atlantic,* January 20, 2017, https://www.theatlantic.com/international/archive/2017/01/trump-edelman-trust-crisis/513350; Matthew Ingram, "Most Trump Supporters Don't Trust the Media Anymore," *Fortune,* February 1, 2017, http://fortune.com/2017/02/01/trump-voters-media-trust; Noah Millman, "Trumpism and the Politics of Distrust," *American Conservative,* August 1, 2017, http://www.theamericanconservative.com/millman/trumpism-and-the-politics-of-distrust; Adam Serwer, "The Nationalist's Delusion," *The Atlantic,* November 20, 2017, https://www.theatlantic.com/politics/archive/2017/11/the-nationalists-delusion/546356; Eugene Scott, "White Working-Class Evangelicals: Christian Values Are under Attack," CNN, September 24, 2016, https://www.cnn.com/2016/09/24/politics/white-working-class-evangelicals/index.html; and Hansi Lo Wang, "Distrust of Government Drove Many New Hampshire Voters to Trump," All Things Considered, NPR, November 14, 2016, https://www.npr.org/2016/11/14/502050969/distrust-of-government-drove-many-new-hampshire-voters-to-trump. For further information on Trump voters' focus on party affiliation, see Thomas Edsall, "Trump Says Jump. His Supporters Ask, How High?" *New York Times,* September 14, 2017, https://www.nytimes.com/2017/09/14/opinion/trump-republicans.html; Ezra Klein, "For Elites, Politics Is Driven by Ideology. For Voters, It's Not," *Vox,* November 9, 2017, https://www.vox.com/policy-and-politics/2017/11/9/16614672/ideology-liberal-conservatives; and John Prideaux, "A Special Report on Donald Trump's America," *The Economist,* July 1, 2017, https://www.economist.com/special-report/2017/07/01/a-special-report-on-donald-trumps-america.

10. Donehower, "How to Reread Appalachian Literacy Research," 14.

11. Weller, *Yesterday's People,* 161, 163.

12. Loyal Jones, *Appalachian Values* (Ashland, KY: Jesse Stuart Foundation, 1994); Weller, *Yesterday's People,* 161–63.

13. Eller, *Uneven Ground,* 41, 101.

14. "Kentucky Highlands Promise Zone," Kentucky Promise Zone, 2016, http://www.kypromisezone.com.

15. Virginia Rinaldo Seitz, *Women, Development, and Communities for Empowerment in Appalachia* (Albany: State University of New York Press, 1995), 120.

16. Todd Snyder, "The Transition to College for First-Generation Students from Extractive Industry Appalachia," in Webb-Sunderhaus and Donehower, eds., *Rereading Appalachian Stereotypes,* 77–99, 78.

17. Webb-Sunderhaus, "'Keep the Appalachian, Drop the Redneck,'" 23.

18. Reid Luhman, "Appalachian English Stereotypes: Language Attitudes in Kentucky," *Language and Society* 19, no. 3 (1990): 331–48, 340; U. Mae Reck, Gregory Reck, and Susan Keefe, "Implications of Teachers' Perceptions of Students in an Appalachian School," *Journal of Research and Development in Education* 26, no. 2 (1993): 117–21, 119–20.

19. James Branscome, "Annihilating the Hillbilly: Appalachians' Struggle with America's Institutions," in *Colonialism in Modern American: The Appalachian Case,* ed. Helen Matthews Lewis, Linda Johnson, and Donald Askins (Boone, NC: Appalachian State University, 1978), 211–28, 217; Kim Donehower, "Literacy Choices in an Appalachian Community," *Journal of Appalachian Studies* 9, no. 2 (2003): 341–62, 346.

20. Donehower, "Literacy Choices in an Appalachian Community," 353–54.

21. Katherine Kelleher Sohn, "Whistlin' and Crowin' Women of Appalachia: Literacy Practices since College," *College Composition and Communication* 54, no. 3 (2003): 423–52, 439.

22. Eller, *Uneven Ground;* William Schumann, "Introduction: Place and Place-Making in Appalachia," in *Appalachia Revisited: New Perspectives on Place, Tradition, and Progress,* ed. William Schumann and Rebecca Adkins Fletcher (Lexington: University Press of Kentucky, 2016), 1–28, 10; Peter Mortensen, "Figuring Illiteracy: Rustic Bodies and Unlettered Minds in Rural America," in *Rhetorical Bodies,* ed. Jack Selzer and Sharon Crowley (Madison: University of Wisconsin Press, 1999), 143–70, 163.

23. Locklear, *Negotiating a Perilous Empowerment,* 24.

24. Anderson, *Imagined Communities,* 6.

25. Harari, *Homo Deus,* 60.

Bibliography

"About *Mountain Advocate*. (Barbourville, Ky.) 1904–1935." Chronicling America: Historic American Newspapers, Library of Congress, 2018. https://chroniclingamerica.loc.gov/lccn/sn87060032.

"About the *Big Sandy News*. (Louisa, Ky.) 1885–1929." Chronicling America: Historic American Newspapers, Library of Congress, 2018. https://chroniclingamerica.loc.gov/lccn/sn83004226.

"About the *Clay City Times*. (Clay City, Ky.) 1901–Current." Chronicling America: Historic American Newspapers, Library of Congress, 2018. https://chroniclingamerica.loc.gov/lccn/sn86069657.

"About the *Hazel Green Herald*. (Hazel Green, Wolfe County, Ky.) 1885–19??." Chronicling America: Historic American Newspapers, Library of Congress, 2018. https://chroniclingamerica.loc.gov/lccn/sn86063242.

Allen, James Lane. *The Blue-Grass Region of Kentucky and Other Kentucky Articles*. New York: Harper & Bros., 1892.

Anderson, Benedict. *Imagined Communities: Reflections on the Origin and Spread of Nationalism*. London: Verso, 1983; reprint, London; Verso, 2016.

Appalachian Regional Commission. "The Appalachian Region." Appalachian Regional Commission, n.d. https://www.arc.gov/appalachian_region/TheAppalachianRegion.asp.

Baker, Kevin. "The Eternal Sunshine of the Spotless White Mind." *New Republic*, March 18, 2017. https://newrepublic.com/article/141435/eternal-sunshine-spotless-white-mind.

Baldwin, Yvonne Honeycutt. *Cora Wilson Stewart and Kentucky's Moonlight Schools: Fighting for Literacy in America*. Lexington: University Press of Kentucky, 2006.

Banker, Mark. *Appalachians All: East Tennesseans and the Elusive History of an American Region*. Knoxville: University of Tennessee Press, 2010.

Batteau, Allen. *The Invention of Appalachia*. Tucson: University of Arizona Press, 1990.

"Be Happy for Coal Miners Losing Their Health Insurance. They're Getting Exactly What They Voted For." Daily Kos, December 12, 2016. https://www.dailykos.com/stories/2016/12/12/1610198/-Be-happy-for-coal-miners-losing-their-health-insurance-They-re-getting-exactly-what-they-voted-for.

Bello, Marisol. "No Victory in War on Poverty in Eastern Kentucky." *USA Today*, January 25, 2014. https://www.usatoday.com/story/news/nation/2014/01/25/war-on-poverty-50th-anniversary/4326109.

Bowles, Sarah Jordan. "Troublesome Inventions: The Rhetoric of the Hindman Settlement School, 1902–1927." PhD diss., Miami University, 2008.

Brandt, Deborah. "Sponsors of Literacy." *College Composition and Communication* 49, no. 2 (1998): 165–85.

———. *Literacy in American Lives*. Cambridge: Cambridge University Press, 2001.

———. *The Rise of Writing: Redefining Mass Literacy*. Cambridge: Cambridge University Press, 2014.

Branscome, James. "Annihilating the Hillbilly: Appalachians' Struggle with America's Institutions." In *Colonialism in Modern American: The Appalachian Case*, ed. Helen Matthews Lewis, Linda Johnson, and Donald Askins, 211–28. Boone, NC: Appalachian State University, 1978.

Brazeau, Alicia. *Circulating Literacy: Writing Instruction in American Periodicals, 1880–1910*. Carbondale: Southern Illinois University Press, 2016.

Bryson, Krista. "Conflicted Rhetorics of Appalachian Identity in the Kentucky Moonlight Schools." In *Rereading Appalachian Stereotypes: Literacy, Place, and Cultural Resistance*, ed. Sara Webb-Sunderhaus and Kim Donehower, 179–98. Lexington: University Press of Kentucky, 2015.

Carian, Emily K., and Tagart Cain Sobotka. "Playing the Trump Card: Masculinity Threat and the U.S. 2016 Presidential Election." *Socius*, January 2018. doi:10.1177/2378023117740699.

Carnes, Nicholas, and Noam Lupu. "It's Time to Bust the Myth: Most Trump Voters Were Not Working Class." *Washington Post*, June 5, 2017. https://www.washingtonpost.com/news/monkey-cage/wp/2017/06/05/its-time-to-bust-the-myth-most-trump-voters-were-not-working-class/?utm_term=.7322a1181e94.

Caudill, Harry. *Night Comes to the Cumberlands: A Biography of a Depressed Area*. New York: Little, Brown, 1963.

Cohen, Roger. "We Need 'Somebody Spectacular': Views from Trump Country." *New York Times*, September 9, 2016. https://www.nytimes.com/2016/09/11/opinion/sunday/we-need-somebody-spectacular-views-from-trump-country.html.

Concise Oxford Companion to American Literature. Edited by James Hart. Oxford: Oxford University Press, 2002.

Conroy, J. Oliver. "'Angry White Men': The Sociologist Who Studied Trump's Base Before Trump." *The Guardian*, February 27, 2017. https://www.theguardian.com/world/2017/feb/27/michael-kimmel-masculinity-far-right-angry-white-men.

Coppins, McKay. "You Need to Think about It Like a War." *The Atlantic*. December 7, 2017. https://www.theatlantic.com/politics/archive/2017/12/the-vanishing-values-voter/547772.

"County Courthouse Disasters in Kentucky." Kentucky Department of Libraries and Archives, 2018. https://kdla.ky.gov/researchers/Pages/courthousedisasters.aspx.

Cox, Daniel, Rachel Lienesch, and Robert Jones. "Beyond Economics: Fears of Cultural Displacement Pushed the White Working Class to Trump." PRRI, May 9, 2017. https://www.prri.org/research/white-working-class-attitudes-economy-trade-immigration-election-donald-trump.

Donehower, Kim. "Literacy Choices in an Appalachian Community." *Journal of Appalachian Studies* 9, no. 2 (2003): 341–62.

———. "How to Reread Appalachian Literacy Research." In *Rereading Appalachia: Literacy, Place, and Cultural Resistance*, ed. Sara Webb-Sunderhaus and Kim Donehower, 13–32. Lexington: University Press of Kentucky, 2015.

Drake, Richard. *A History of Appalachia*. Lexington: University Press of Kentucky, 2001.

Edsall, Thomas. "Trump Says Jump. His Supporters Ask, How High?" *New York Times*, September 14, 2017. https://www.nytimes.com/2017/09/14/opinion/trump-republicans.html.

Edwards-Levy, Ariel. "Americans Don't Think the Government Needs 'Experts.'" *Huffington Post*, December 8, 2016. https://www.huffingtonpost.com/entry/poll-civil-service-experts_us_5849d515e4b04c8e2baeede9.

Ekins, Emily. "The Five Types of Trump Voters: Who They Are and What They Believe." Democracy Fund Voter Study Group, June 2017. https://www.voterstudygroup.org/publications/2016-elections/the-five-types-trump-voters.

Eller, Ronald D. Foreword to *Back Talk from Appalachia: Confronting Stereotypes*, ed. Dwight B. Billings, Gurney Norman, and Katherine Ledford, ix–xi. Lexington: University Press of Kentucky, 1999.

———. *Uneven Ground: Appalachia since 1945*. Lexington: University Press of Kentucky, 2008.

Ellis, William. *A History of Education in Kentucky*. Lexington: University Press of Kentucky, 2011.

Engelhardt, Elizabeth. "Writing That Old Moonshine Lit: Gender, Power, and Nation in Unexpected Places." *Journal of Appalachian Studies* 13, nos. 1–2 (2007): 49–74.

Enoch, Jessica. *Refiguring Rhetorical Education: Women Teaching African American, Native American, and Chicano/a Students, 1865–1911*. Carbondale: Southern Illinois University Press, 2008.

Erickson, Phillip. "Baylor Researchers Examine Trump Voters, Religious Values." *Waco Tribune-Herald*, September 7, 2017. http://www.wacotrib.com/news/higher education/baylor-researchers-examine-trump-voters-religious-values/article_24adfb74-64a3-5543-a11a-5580856b7229.html.

Evans, Herndon J. *The Newspaper Press of Kentucky*. Lexington: University Press of Kentucky, 1976; reprint, Lexington: University Press of Kentucky, 2009.

Ferrell, Ann. "'It's Really Hard to Tell the True Story of Tobacco': Stigma, Tellability, and Reflexive Scholarship." *Journal of Folklore Research* 49, no. 2 (2012): 127–52.

Filipovic, Jill. "What Donald Trump Thinks It Takes to Be a Man." *New York Times*, November 2, 2018. https://www.nytimes.com/2017/11/02/opinion/sunday/donald-trump-masculinity.html.

Fording, Richard, and Sanford Schram. "The Cognitive and Emotional Sources of Trump Support: The Case of Low-Information Voters." *New Political Science* 39, no. 4 (2017): 670–86.

Fox, John, Jr. *The Kentuckians: A Knight of the Cumberland*. New York: Scribner, 1909.

Friedman, Uri. "Why Trump Is Thriving in an Age of Distrust." *The Atlantic*, January 20, 2017. https://www.theatlantic.com/international/archive/2017/01/trump-edelman-trust-crisis/513350.

Gabriele, Sandra, and Paul Moore. "The *Globe* on Saturday, the *World* on Sunday: Toronto Weekend Editions and the Influence of the American Sunday Paper, 1886–1895." *Canadian Journal of Communication* 34, no. 3 (2009): 337–58.

Galofaro, Claire. "In the Heart of Trump Country, His Base's Faith Is Unshaken." AP News, December 28, 2017. https://apnews.com/ee19ceb7cf0d4af4ab73c393708148bf.

Gilliam Fisher, Diane. *Kettle Bottom*. Florence, MA: Perugia, 2004.

Graff, Harvey. *The Legacies of Literacy: Continuities and Contradictions in Western Culture and Society*. Bloomington: Indiana University Press, 1991.

———. *The Literacy Myth: Cultural Integration and Social Structure in the Nineteenth Century*. New York: Academic, 1979; reprint, New York: Routledge, 2017.

Greer, Jane. "Expanding Working-Class Rhetorical Traditions: The Moonlight Schools and Alternative Solidarities among Appalachian Women, 1911–1920." *College English* 77, no. 3 (2015): 216–35.

Hagedorn, Elizabeth. "This Is What Victory Looks Like in the Most Pro-Trump County in America." *Circa*, November 9, 2016. https://www.circa.com/story/2016/11/09/politics/this-is-what-victory-looks-like-in-the-most-pro-trump-county-in-america (link no longer active).

Harari, Yuval Noah. *Sapiens: A Brief History of Humankind*. New York: Harper's, 2015.

———. *Homo Deus: A Brief History of Tomorrow*. New York: Harper's, 2017.

Howse, Emma. "Appalachian Identities and the Difficulties of Archival Literacy Research." In *Rereading Appalachian Stereotypes: Literacy, Place, and Cultural Resistance*, ed. Sara Webb-Sunderhaus and Kim Donehower, 55–76. Lexington: University Press of Kentucky, 2015.

Hutton, T. R. C. *Bloody Breathitt: Politics and Violence in the Appalachian South*. Lexington: University Press of Kentucky, 2015.

Ingram, Mathew. "Most Trump Supporters Don't Trust the Media Anymore." *Fortune*, February 1, 2017. http://fortune.com/2017/02/01/trump-voters-media-trust.

Jacobs, Tom. "Inside the Mind of Hardcore Trump Supporters." *Pacific Standard*, February 15, 2018. https://psmag.com/news/inside-the-minds-of-hardcore-trump-supporters.

Johnson, Paul Elliott. "The Art of Masculine Victimhood: Donald Trump's Demagoguery." *Women's Studies in Communication* 40, no. 3 (2017): 229–50.

Jones, Calvin P. "National Register of Historic Places Inventory—Nomination Form." US Department of the Interior, 1978. https://npgallery.nps.gov/NRHP/GetAsset/NRHP/79001047_text.

Jones, Loyal. *Appalachian Values*. Ashland, KY: Jesse Stuart Foundation, 1994.

Kahn, Patricia. "How the Social Reform Movement Impacted Handiwork at Hindman Settlement School in Hindman, Kentucky during 1902–1920." PhD diss., Ohio State University, 2003.

Kazan, Olga. "The Precarious Masculinity of 2016 Voters." *The Atlantic*, October 12, 2016. https://www.theatlantic.com/politics/archive/2016/10/male-trump-voters-masculinity/503741.

Keefe, Dennis. "Andragogy in the Appalachians: Myles Horton, the Highlander Folk

School, and Education for Social and Economic Justice." *International Journal of Adult Vocational Education and Technology* 6, no. 3 (2015): 16–30.

Keeney, Charles B. "The Battle of Blair Mountain Is Still Being Waged." Cultural Landscape Foundation, February 26, 2018. https://tclf.org/battle-blair-mountain-still-being-waged.

"Kentucky Highlands Promise Zone." Kentucky Promise Zone, 2016. http://www.kypromisezone.com.

Klein, Ezra. "For Elites, Politics Is Driven by Ideology. For Voters, It's Not." *Vox*, November 9, 2017. https://www.vox.com/policy-and-politics/2017/11/9/16614672/ideology-liberal-conservatives.

Kolko, Jed. "Trump Was Stronger Where the Economy Is Weaker." *FiveThirtyEight*, November 10, 2016. https://fivethirtyeight.com/features/trump-was-stronger-where-the-economy-is-weaker.

Lewis, Ronald. *Transforming the Appalachian Countryside: Railroads, Deforestation, and Social Change in West Virginia, 1880–1920*. Chapel Hill: University of North Carolina Press, 1998.

———. "Beyond Isolation and Homogeneity: Diversity and the History of Appalachia." In *Back Talk from Appalachia: Confronting Stereotypes*, ed. Dwight B. Billings, Gurney Norman, and Katherine Ledford, 21–44. Lexington: University Press of Kentucky, 1999.

Locklear, Erica Abrams. *Negotiating a Perilous Empowerment: Appalachian Women's Literacies*. Athens: Ohio University Press, 2011.

Looff, David. *Appalachia's Children: The Challenge of Mental Health*. Lexington: University Press of Kentucky, 1971.

Luhman, Reid. "Appalachian English Stereotypes: Language Attitudes in Kentucky." *Language and Society* 19, no. 3 (1990): 331–48.

Marshall, Catherine. *Christy*. New York: McGraw-Hill, 1967.

McGreal, Chris. "America's Poorest White Town: Abandoned by Coal, Swallowed by Drugs." *The Guardian*, November 12, 2015. https://www.theguardian.com/us-news/2015/nov/12/beattyville-kentucky-and-americas-poorest-towns.

Millman, Noah. "Trumpism and the Politics of Distrust." *American Conservative*, August 1, 2017. http://www.theamericanconservative.com/millman/trumpism-and-the-politics-of-distrust.

Mortensen, Peter. "Figuring Illiteracy: Rustic Bodies and Unlettered Minds in Rural America." In *Rhetorical Bodies*, ed. Jack Selzer and Sharon Crowley, 143–70. Madison: University of Wisconsin Press, 1999.

Motta, Matt. "Had Enough of Experts? Anti-Intellectualism Is Linked to Voters' Support for Movements That Are Skeptical of Expertise." LSE USCentre, August 30, 2017. http://blogs.lse.ac.uk/usappblog/2017/08/30/had-enough-of-experts-anti-intellectualism-is-linked-to-voters-support-for-movements-that-are-skeptical-of-expertise.

Murfree, Mary Noailles. *In the Tennessee Mountains*. London: Longmans, Green, 1884.

Mutz, Diana. "Status Threat, Not Economic Hardship, Explains 2016 Presidential Vote."

Proceedings of the National Academy of Sciences of the United States of America, vol. 115, no. 19 (2018). http://www.pnas.org/content/115/19/E4330.

NeCamp, Samantha. "The *Hazel Green Herald* and the 'Idea of Appalachia.'" *Journal of Appalachian Studies* 17, no. 2 (2011): 66–84.

———. *Adult Literacy and American Identity: The Moonlight Schools and Americanization Programs*. Carbondale: Southern Illinois University Press, 2014.

Nelms, Willie. *Cora Wilson Stewart: Crusader against Illiteracy*. Jefferson, NC: McFarland, 1997.

Nichols, Tom. "Trump Is Delivering What He Promised: A Government with No Experts." *Washington Post*, March 8, 2018. https://www.washingtonpost.com/news/posteverything/wp/2018/03/08/president-trump-is-delivering-what-he-promised-a-government-with-no-experts/?utm_term=.4a0a61c4449e.

Okker, Patricia. *Social Stories: The Magazine Novel in Nineteenth-Century America*. Charlottesville: University of Virginia Press, 2003.

Osthaus, Carl. *Partisans of the Southern Press: Editorial Spokesmen of the Nineteenth Century*. Lexington: University Press of Kentucky, 1994.

Parins, James. *Literacy and Intellectual Life in the Cherokee Nation, 1820–1906*. Norman: University of Oklahoma Press, 2013.

Payne, George. *History of Journalism in the United States*. New York: D. Appleton, 1924.

Pearce, John Ed. *Days of Darkness: The Feuds of Eastern Kentucky*. Lexington: University Press of Kentucky, 1994.

Pedersen, Sarah. "What's in a Name? The Revealing Use of Nom de Plumes in Women's Correspondence to Daily Newspapers in Edwardian Scotland." *Media History* 10, no. 3 (2004): 175–85.

Plein, Stewart. "Portraits of Appalachia: The Identification of Stereotype in Publisher's Bookbindings, 1850–1915." *Journal of Appalachian Studies* 15, nos. 1–2 (2009): 99–115.

Prideaux, John. "A Special Report on Donald Trump's America." *The Economist*, July 1, 2017. https://www.economist.com/special-report/2017/07/01/a-special-report-on-donald-trumps-america.

Prior, Paul, and Jody Shipka. "Chronotopic Lamination: Tracing the Contours of Literate Activity." In *Writing Selves/Writing Societies*, ed. Charles Bazerman and David Russell, 180–237. Fort Collins, CO: WAC Clearinghouse, 2003. https://wac.colostate.edu/books/perspectives/selves-societies.

Pudup, Mary Beth, Dwight Billings, and Altina Waller. *Appalachia in the Making: The Mountain South in the Nineteenth Century*. Chapel Hill: University of North Carolina Press, 1995.

Purcell-Gates, Victoria. *Other People's Words: The Cycle of Low Literacy*. Cambridge, MA: Harvard University Press, 1995.

Reck, U. Mae, Gregory Reck, and Susan Keefe. "Implications of Teachers' Perceptions of Students in an Appalachian School." *Journal of Research and Development in Education* 26, no. 2 (1993): 117–21.

Rich, Frank. "No Sympathy for the Hillbilly." *New York Magazine*, March 9, 2017. http://

nymag.com/daily/intelligencer/2017/03/frank-rich-no-sympathy-for-the-hillbilly.html.

Riotta, Chris. "Majority of Republicans Say Colleges Are Bad for America (Yes, Really!)." *Newsweek*, July 10, 2017. http://www.newsweek.com/republicans-believe-college-education-bad-america-donald-trump-media-fake-news-634474.

Rivas, Javier. "Our Experiment into How Voters Think Shows That They Go with Their Guts." *The Conversation*, January 18, 2018. http://theconversation.com/our-experiment-into-how-voters-think-shows-that-they-go-with-their-guts-90241.

Rodd, Scott. "This Is What Poverty Looks Like." *ThinkProgress*, March 11, 2015. https://thinkprogress.org/this-is-what-poverty-looks-like-5218e194d4fe.

Saward, Jeff. "Welcome to Trump Country, U.S.A." *Vanity Fair*, February 24, 2016. https://www.vanityfair.com/news/2016/02/donald-trump-supporters-west-virginia.

Schenkkan, Robert. *The Kentucky Cycle*. New York: Plume, 1992.

Schneider, Stephen. *You Can't Padlock an Idea: Rhetorical Education at the Highlander Folk School, 1932–1961*. Columbia: University of South Carolina Press, 2014.

Schudson, Michael. "Toward a Troubleshooting Manual for Journalism History." *Journalism and Mass Communication Quarterly* 74, no. 3 (1997): 463–76.

Schumann, William. "Introduction: Place and Place-Making in Appalachia." In *Appalachia Revisited: New Perspectives on Place, Tradition, and Progress*, ed. William Schumann and Rebecca Adkins Fletcher, 1–28. Lexington: University Press of Kentucky, 2016.

Scott, Eugene. "White Working-Class Evangelicals: Christian Values Are under Attack." CNN, September 24, 2016. https://www.cnn.com/2016/09/24/politics/white-working-class-evangelicals/index.html.

Seitz, Virginia Rinaldo. *Women, Development, and Communities for Empowerment in Appalachia*. Albany: State University of New York Press, 1995.

Serwer, Adam. "The Nationalist's Delusion." *The Atlantic*, November 20, 2017. https://www.theatlantic.com/politics/archive/2017/11/the-nationalists-delusion/546356.

Shapiro, Henry. *Appalachia on Our Mind: The Southern Mountains and the Mountaineer in the American Consciousness, 1870–1920*. Chapel Hill: University of North Carolina Press, 1978.

Sherman, Ryne. "Personal Values and Support for Donald Trump during the 2016 US Presidential Primary." *Personality and Individual Differences* 128, no. 1 (2018): 33–38.

Shuman, Amy. *Other People's Stories: Entitlement Claims and the Critique of Empathy*. Urbana: University of Illinois Press, 2010.

Sinor, Jennifer. *The Extraordinary Work of Ordinary Writing: Annie Ray's Diary*. Iowa City: University of Iowa Press, 2002.

Smith, Lee. *Fair and Tender Ladies*. New York: Pan, 1988.

Snyder, Todd. "The Transition to College for First-Generation Students from Extractive Industry Appalachia." In *Rereading Appalachian Stereotypes: Literacy, Place, and Cultural Resistance*, ed. Sara Webb-Sunderhaus and Kim Donehower, 77–99. Lexington: University Press of Kentucky, 2015.

Sohn, Katherine Kelleher. "Whistlin' and Crowin' Women of Appalachia: Literacy

Practices since College." *College Composition and Communication* 54, no. 3 (2003): 423–52.

Soltow, Lee, and Edward Stevens. *The Rise of Literacy and the Common School in the United States: A Socioeconomic Analysis to 1870*. Chicago: University of Chicago Press, 1981.

Soltz, Wendy. "Just Miles Away but Worlds Apart: Examining Jewish Participation in Integration Programs at Black Mountain College and Highlander Folk School, 1933–1964." *Association for Jewish Studies Review* 41, no. 1 (2017): 203–33.

Soodalter, Ron. "In the Battle of Blair Mountain, Coal Is Threatening to Bury Labor History." *The Progressive*, January 31, 2018. http://progressive.org/magazine/the-battle-over-blair-mountain-famous-labor-site.

Stewart, Cora Wilson. *Moonlight Schools: For the Emancipation of Adult Illiterates*. New York: Dutton, 1922.

Stoddart, Jess. *The Quare Women's Journals: May Stone and Katherine Pettit's Summers in the Kentucky Mountains and the Founding of the Hindman Settlement School*. Frankfort, KY: Jesse Stuart Foundation, 1997.

———. *Challenge and Change in Appalachia: The Story of the Hindman Settlement School*. Lexington: University Press of Kentucky, 2002.

Thayer-Bacon, Barbara J. "An Exploration of Myles Horton's Democratic Praxis: Highlander Folk School." *Journal of Educational Foundations* 18, no. 2, (2004): 5–23.

Tocqueville, Alexis de. *Democracy in America*. Translated by Arthur Goldhammer. New York: Penguin Putnam, 2004.

Toynbee, Arnold. *A Study of History: Abridgment of Volumes I–VI by D. C. Somervell*. Oxford: Oxford University Press, 1947.

"2016 General Election Turnout." West Virginia Secretary of State Office, 2018. https://sos.wv.gov/elections/Documents/HistVoteTurnoutDocs/2016General.pdf.

"2016 West Virginia Presidential Election Results." *Politico*, December 13, 2016. https://www.politico.com/2016-election/results/map/president/west-virginia.

US Census Bureau. *1880 Census*. Washington, DC: National Archives and Records Administration, 1880. https://search.ancestry.com/search/db.aspx?dbid=6742.

———. *1900 Census*. Washington, DC: National Archives and Records Administration, 1900. https://search.ancestry.com/search/db.aspx?dbid=7602.

Vance, J. D. *Hillbilly Elegy: A Memoir of a Family and Culture in Crisis*. New York: Harper, 2016.

Vance, Rupert. "An Introductory Note." In *Yesterday's People: Life in Contemporary Appalachia*, by Jack Weller, ix–xii. Lexington: University Press of Kentucky, 1965; reprint, Lexington: University Press of Kentucky, 2013.

Wallace, Gregory. "Voter Turnout at 20-Year Low in 2016." CNN, November 30, 2016. https://www.cnn.com/2016/11/11/politics/popular-vote-turnout-2016/index.html.

Waller, Altina. *Feud: Hatfields, McCoys, and Social Change in Appalachia, 1860–1900*. Chapel Hill: University of North Carolina Press, 1988.

Wang, Hansi Lo. "Distrust of Government Drove Many New Hampshire Voters to

Trump." All Things Considered, NPR, November 14, 2016. https://www.npr.org/2016/11/14/502050969/distrust-of-government-drove-many-new-hampshire-voters-to-trump.

Webb-Sunderhaus, Sara. "Rhetorical Theories of Appalachian Literacies." In *Rereading Appalachian Stereotypes: Literacy, Place, and Cultural Resistance*, ed. Sara Webb-Sunderhaus and Kim Donehower, 179–98. Lexington: University Press of Kentucky, 2015.

———. "'Keep the Appalachian, Drop the Redneck': Tellable Student Narratives of Appalachian Identity." *College English* 73, no. 1 (2016): 11–33.

Weller, Jack. *Yesterday's People: Life in Contemporary Appalachia*. Lexington: University Press of Kentucky, 1965; reprint, Lexington: University Press of Kentucky, 2013.

West, David. "The Economic Anxiety That Helped Fuel Trump's Rise Isn't Going Away, and Neither Is Trumpism." NBC News, April 21, 2018. https://www.nbcnews.com/think/opinion/economic-anxiety-helped-fuel-trump-s-rise-isn-t-going-ncna866816.

Whisnant, David. *All That Is Native and Fine: The Politics of Culture in an American Region*. Chapel Hill: University of North Carolina Press, 1984.

Williams, John. "Counting Yesterday's People: Using Aggregate Data to Address the Problem of Appalachia's Boundaries." *Journal of Appalachian Studies* 2, no. 1 (1996): 3–27.

———. *Appalachia: A History*. Chapel Hill: University North Carolina Press, 2002.

Index

advertisements, 11, 17, 28, 29, 33, 39–41; of Caleb Powers's memoir, 43–44; as a source of income, 10, 27
African Americans: as audience members, 33–34; violence toward, 67–68
Appalachia: boundaries of, 14; perceptions of illiteracy in, 5–6, 71–72, 73; universality of descriptions of, 15–16
Appalachian Regional Commission, 14–15
archival research, difficulty of, 5–7

Barbourville, Kentucky, 21, 28, 29
Bible, the, 30–31, 41
Big Sandy News, 17, 30–31, 33–35, 40, 42, 45; continued existence of, 47; correspondents in, 54–56, 57, 58–59; discussions of schooling in, 75, 79, 82, 83, 84–87, 90; establishment of, 19; letters to the editor in, 64–65; politics of, 17, 19, 44
Blair Mountain, Battle of, 6–7, 14
Bloody Breathitt, 22–23
Breathitt County News, 16, 38–39, 42, 46, 51, 67, 68–69; discussion of schooling in, 79, 88–89; establishment of, 23, 28; letters to the editor in, 63–64; politics of, 17, 34, 64
Burgher, J. E., 22, 27, 29–30, 33, 36, 43–45, 65–66, 67, 82, 87–88; relationship with correspondents, 50–51, 54, 56, 57; as writer, 67–68; 69–70
Burman, Fred, 22, 37–38, 52

central Appalachia, boundaries of, 14–16
Christy, 73, 74
Clark, Daniel, 21, 29–30, 36; as writer, 70
Clay City, Kentucky, 17, 22, 79–80
Clay City Times, 17, 31–33, 67, 69–70; continued existence of, 47; correspondents for, 50–51, 52, 54, 56, 57, 60–61; discussion of schooling in, 75–77, 78, 79–80, 81, 82, 87; establishment of, 22–23, 27; letters to the editor in, 65; politics of, 17, 34, 39, 43–44, 67
coal. *See* extract industries
Cole, Charles, 21
common schools. *See* public schools
Conley, Milton, 19, 30–31, 33–36, 44, 87–88; relationship with correspondents, 54–56, 57
Cooper, Spencer, 20, 27, 29–30, 32, 35–36, 38, 88; relationship with correspondents, 51
correspondents, 74, 90; as businessmen, 52–53; editors' calls for, 50–52; interactions with one another, 58–62; use of pen names by, 53, 57, 59–60
cycle, idea of, 8, 95–96, 101, 105, 109, 110–11, 112

editors: as arbiters of reading practices, 34–35, 41, 42–44, 45–46; role in shaping news, 35–37, 54–58; as sponsors of literacy, 10–11, 23, 27–28, 47; as writers, 66
extract industries, 5–6, 8, 13, 15, 89, 96, 101, 109, 111

fatalism, 96, 98
feuds: in Breathitt County, 23–24, 64, 67, 68–69; as a feature of the idea of Appalachia, 2, 4, 72; French-Eversole, 64

Goebel, William, 21, 24, 43

Hagin, J. Wise, 24, 28, 64, 111; as writer, 68–69

Hargis, James, 24
Hatfield, Sid, 14
Hazel Green, Kentucky, 20
Hazel Green Academy, 20, 21
Hazel Green Herald, 16, 29, 31, 33, 35–36, 38, 40–42, 44; correspondents for, 51, 52, 61–62; discussions of schooling in, 81, 83, 88, 90–91; establishment of: 20, 27; politics of, 17, 20, 34, 45
Highlander Folk School, 73
Hindman Settlement School, 26, 73, 91, 92

idea of Appalachia, 11, 13–14; 15; 23, 40; 46, 71–72; 73, 80, 92–93; definition of, 2, 4–8; 49; direct responses to, 68, 77; effects of, 94–97, 100, 103, 105–12
imagined community, 16–17, 28, 33, 34–35, 49; definition of, 9–10

Jones, Loyal, 103

letters to the editor, 62–66
literacy: definition of, 17–18; literacy myth: 49, 89. *See also* sponsorship of literacy
local color writing, 5, 13, 15
Louisa, Kentucky, 19–20
Louisa Normal School, 19–20

Matewan, West Virginia, 14
McDonald, W. H., 22, 36
Moonlight Schools, 5, 73, 91
Mountain Advocate, 17, 32–34, 36, 37–38, 40, 43, 67; continued existence of, 47; correspondents for, 51, 52, 54–55, 59–60; discussions of schooling in, 76, 82, 83, 90–91; establishment of, 21–22, 28, 29; letters to the editor in, 62–63; politics of, 17, 39, 62–63, 70

newspapers: club rates for, 39–40; "discourse of need" in development of, 27–28; economic benefits of, 38–39; importance for community development, 8–9, 28, 49; intended audiences for, 33–34; moral and educational benefits of, 32, 46; political leanings of, 17, 34; subscription payments to, 30–32, 33

O'Mara, M. P, 22

Pine Mountain Settlement School, 26, 73
Powers, Caleb, 21, 43–44, 62–63
public schools, 74, 81, 86; community support for, 75–76, 86; funding of, 75, 77, 78, 81; low attendance figures for, 78, 79–80

roads. *See* travel, difficulty of

schooling: Appalachian attitudes toward, 73–74, 75–77, 80, 87–88, 89–92, 104; negative stereotypes encountered by students in, 105–9; representations of by outsiders, 73, 77
serialized stories, 42
sponsorship of literacy, 26; editors as sponsors, 10–11, 23, 27–28, 47, 90; definition of, 10
Spout Spring Times, 22, 42; establishment of, 22, 27
subscription schools, 74, 78–80, 81, 86

teachers: fraud in examinations of, 83; pay, 75, 82–83; selection of, 81–82, 83–86
tellability, 96–97, 109
Torchlight community school, 77, 78, 111
travel, difficulty of, 53–54, 76–77, 80–81
Trump, Donald: Appalachia as "Trump Country," 1–3, 101–2; votes for, 2–3, 104
Trump Country. *See* Trump, Donald

Union College, 21

War on Poverty, 26, 98, 100, 103
Weller, Jack, 97–103, 110
women: as readers, 33; as writers, 53

Yesterday's People. See Weller, Jack

PLACE MATTERS: NEW DIRECTIONS IN APPALACHIAN STUDIES

SERIES EDITOR: Dwight B. Billings

This series explores the history, social life, and cultures of Appalachia from multidisciplinary, comparative, and global perspectives. Topics include geography, the environment, public policy, political economy, critical regional studies, diversity, social inequality, social movements and activism, migration and immigration, efforts to confront regional stereotypes, literature and the arts, and the ongoing social construction and reimagination of Appalachia. Key goals of the series are to place Appalachian dynamics in the context of global change and to demonstrate that place-based and regional studies still matter.

Appalachia in Regional Context: Place Matters
Edited by Dwight B. Billings and Ann E. Kingsolver

Literacy in the Mountains: Community, Newspapers, and Writing in Appalachia
Samantha NeCamp

Appalachia Revisited: New Perspectives on Place, Tradition, and Progress
Edited by William Schumann and Rebecca Adkins Fletcher

The Arthurdale Community School: Education and Reform in Depression Era Appalachia
Sam F. Stack Jr.

Sacred Mountains: A Christian Ethical Approach to Mountaintop Removal
Andrew R. H. Thompson

Rereading Appalachia: Literacy, Place, and Cultural Resistance
Edited by Sara Webb-Sunderhaus and Kim Donehower

Religion and Resistance in Appalachia: Faith and the Fight against Mountaintop Removal Coal Mining
Joseph D. Witt

CPSIA information can be obtained
at www.ICGtesting.com
Printed in the USA
BVHW032114120120
569031BV00002B/2/P